O9-BUA-143

Gretchen Bitterlin
Dennis Johnson
Donna Price
Sylvia Ramirez
K. Lynn Savage, Series Editor

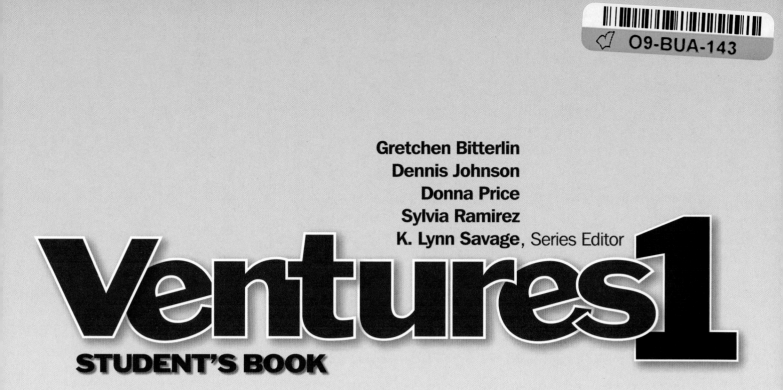

Ventures 1

STUDENT'S BOOK

CAMBRIDGE
UNIVERSITY PRESS

CAMBRIDGE UNIVERSITY PRESS
Cambridge, New York, Melbourne, Madrid, Cape Town, Singapore, São Paulo, Delhi

Cambridge University Press
32 Avenue of the Americas, New York, NY 10013–2473, USA

www.cambridge.org
Information on this title: www.cambridge.org/9780521548380

© Cambridge University Press 2007

This publication is in copyright. Subject to statutory exception
and to the provisions of relevant collective licensing agreements,
no reproduction of any part may take place without the written
permission of Cambridge University Press.

First published 2007
3rd printing 2007

Printed in the United States of America

A catalog record for this publication is available from the British Library

ISBN 978-0-521-54838-0 pack consisting of Student's Book and Audio CD
ISBN 978-0-521-67958-9 Workbook
ISBN 978-0-521-68314-2 pack consisting of Teacher's Edition and Teacher's Toolkit Audio CD / CD-ROM
ISBN 978-0-521-67726-4 CDs (Audio)
ISBN 978-0-521-67727-1 Cassettes
ISBN 978-0-521-67583-3 Add Ventures

Cambridge University Press has no responsibility for
the persistence or accuracy of URLs for external or
third-party Internet Web sites referred to in this publication
and does not guarantee that any content on such
Web sites is, or will remain, accurate or appropriate.

Art direction, book design, photo research, and layout services: Adventure House, NYC
Audio production: Richard LePage & Associates

Authors' acknowledgments

The authors would like to acknowledge and thank focus group participants and reviewers for their insightful comments, as well as CUP editorial, marketing, and production staffs, whose thorough research and attention to detail have resulted in a quality product.

The publishers would also like to extend their particular thanks to the following reviewers and consultants for their valuable insights and suggestions:

Francesca Armendaris, North Orange County Community College District, Anaheim, California; **Alex A. Baez**, The Texas Professional Development Group, Austin, Texas; **Kit Bell**, LAUSD Division of Adult and Career Education, Los Angeles, California; **Rose Anne Cleary**, Catholic Migration Office, Diocese of Brooklyn, Brooklyn, New York; **Inga Cristi**, Pima Community College Adult Education, Tucson, Arizona; **Kay De Gennaro**, West Valley Occupational Center, Woodland Hills, California; **Patricia DeJesus-Lopez**, Illinois Community College Board, Springfield, Illinois; **Magali Apareaida Morais Duignan**, Augusta State University, Augusta, Georgia; **Gayle Fagan**, Harris County Department of Education, Houston, Texas; **Lisa A. Fears**, Inglewood Community Adult School, Inglewood, California; **Jas Gill**, English Language Institute at the University of British Columbia, Vancouver, British Columbia, Canada; **Elisabeth Goodwin**, Pima Community College Adult Education, Tucson, Arizona; **Carolyn Grimaldi**, Center for Immigrant Education and Training, LaGuardia Community College, Long Island City, New York; **Masha Gromyko**, Pima Community College Adult Education, Tucson, Arizona; **Jennifer M. Herrin**, Albuquerque TVI Community College, Albuquerque, New Mexico; **Giang T. Hoang**, Evans Community Adult School, Los Angeles, California; **Karen Hribar**, LAUSD West Valley Occupational Center, Los Angeles, California; **Patricia Ishill**, Union County College, Union County, New Jersey; **Dr. Stephen G. Karel**, McKinley Community School for Adults, Honolulu, Hawaii; **Aaron Kelly**, North Orange County Community College District, Anaheim, California; **Dan Kiernan**, Metro Skills Center, LAUSD, Los Angeles, California; **Kirsten Kilcup**, Green River Community College, Auburn, Washington; **Tom Knutson**, New York Association for New Americans, Inc., New York, New York; **Liz Koenig-Golombek**, LAUSD, Los Angeles, California; **Anita Lemonis**, West Valley Occupational Center, Los Angeles, California; **Lia Lerner**, Burbank Adult School, Burbank, California; **Susan Lundquist**, Pima Community College Adult Education, Tucson, Arizona; **Dr. Amal Mahmoud**, Highline Community College, Des Moines, Washington; **Fatiha Makloufi**, Hostos Community College, Bronx, New York; **Judith Martin-Hall**, Indian River Community College, Fort Pierce, Florida; **Gwen Mayer**, Van Nuys Community Adult School, Los Angeles, California; **Lois Miller**, Pima Community College, Tucson, Arizona; **Vicki Moore**, El Monte-Rosemead Adult School, El Monte, California; **Jeanne Petrus-Rivera**, Cuyahoga Community College, Cleveland, Ohio; **Pearl W. Pigott**, Houston Community College, Houston, Texas; **Catherine Porter**, Adult Learning Resource Center, Des Plaines, Illinois; **Planaria Price**, Evans Community Adult School, Los Angeles, California; **James P. Regan**, NYC Board of Education, New York, New York; **Catherine M. Rifkin**, Florida Community College at Jacksonville, Jacksonville, Florida; **Amy Schneider**, Pacoima Skills Center, Los Angeles, California; **Bonnie Sherman**, Green River Community College, Auburn, Washington; **Julie Singer**, Garfield Community Adult School, Los Angeles, California; **Yilin Sun**, Seattle Central Community College, Seattle, Washington; **André Sutton**, Belmont Community Adult School, Los Angeles, California; **Deborah Thompson**, El Camino Real Community Adult School, Los Angeles, California; **Evelyn Trottier**, Basic Studies Division, Seattle Central Community College, Seattle, Washington; **Debra Un**, New York University, American Language Institute, New York, New York; **Jodie Morgan Vargas**, Orange County Public Schools, Orlando, Florida; **Christopher Wahl**, Hudson County Community College, Jersey City, New Jersey; **Ethel S. Watson**, Evans Community Adult School, Los Angeles, California; **Barbara Williams**; **Mimi Yang**, Belmont Community Adult School, Los Angeles, California; **Adèle Youmans**, Pima Community College Adult Education, Tucson, Arizona.

Scope and sequence

UNIT TITLE TOPIC	FUNCTIONS	LISTENING AND SPEAKING	VOCABULARY	GRAMMAR FOCUS
Welcome Unit pages 2–5	• Identifying the letters of the alphabet • Identifying numbers • Identifying days and months	• Saying the alphabet and numbers • Clarifying spelling • Saying days and months	• The alphabet with capital and lowercase letters • Numbers • Months and days • Holidays	
Unit 1 **Personal information** pages 6–17 **Topic:** Introductions	• Identifying names • Identifying numbers • Using greetings • Identifying countries of origin • Exchanging personal information	• Clarifying spelling • Using greetings • Using appropriate language to introduce self and others	• Personal information • Countries and nationalities • Personal titles	• Possessive adjectives • Subject pronouns • Simple present of *be* • Contractions
Unit 2 **At school** pages 18–29 **Topic:** The classroom	• Describing location • Finding out location	• Asking and giving location of things • Saying *excuse me*	• Classroom furniture • Classroom objects	• Prepositions of location (*in, on*) • *Where is?* • Singular and plural nouns • *Yes / No* questions • Contractions
Review: Units 1 and 2 pages 30–31		• Understanding a conversation		
Unit 3 **Friends and family** pages 32–43 **Topic:** Family	• Describing actions • Talking about family members	• Asking and answering questions about current activities • Answering questions about your family	• Family relationships • Daily activities • Descriptive adjectives	• Present continuous • *Wh-* questions • *Yes / No* questions
Unit 4 **Health** pages 44–55 **Topic:** Health problems	• Describing health problems and suggesting remedies • Expressing sympathy	• Asking about someone's health • Expressing sympathy • Suggesting a remedy	• Body parts • Health problems • Descriptive adjectives	• Simple present of *have* • Questions with *have* • Contractions
Review: Units 3 and 4 pages 56–57		• Understanding a narrative		
Unit 5 **Around town** pages 58–69 **Topic:** Places and directions	• Describing location • Giving directions • Asking for directions • Confirming by repetition	• Asking about a location • Describing your neighborhood • Clarifying directions	• Building and place names • Imperatives for directions	• Prepositions of location (*on, next to, across from, between, on the corner of*) • *Where* questions • Imperatives

READING	WRITING	LIFE SKILLS	PRONUNCIATION
• Reading the alphabet • Reading numbers	• Writing the alphabet • Writing numbers	• Understanding dates • Understanding holidays	• Pronouncing the alphabet • Pronouncing numbers
• Reading a paragraph describing a student's personal information	• Writing sentences giving personal information • Identifying and using capital letters • Understanding alphabetical order	• Reading a registration form • Understanding cultural differences in names • Using personal titles • Using a directory • Reading an ID card	• Pronouncing key vocabulary • Saying telephone numbers • Saying addresses
• Reading sentences describing a classroom • Using pictorial cues	• Writing sentences about the location of items in the classroom • Using capitalization and periods	• Reading an inventory list • Counting objects	• Pronouncing key vocabulary
			• Recognizing syllables
• Reading a paragraph describing a family birthday party • Using a passage's title for comprehension	• Writing sentences about your own family • Writing number words	• Completing an insurance application form • Using family trees • Using formal and informal family titles	• Pronouncing key vocabulary
• Reading a paragraph describing a sick family's visit to a health clinic • Interpreting exclamation points	• Writing an absence note to a child's teacher • Writing dates	• Using an appointment card • Matching remedies to ailments • Showing concern for someone's health	• Pronouncing key vocabulary
			• Pronouncing strong syllables
• Reading a personal letter describing a neighborhood • Interpreting pronoun referents	• Writing a description of your neighborhood • Capitalizing proper nouns	• Reading and drawing maps • Giving and getting directions • Understanding what a DMV is	• Pronouncing key vocabulary

UNIT TITLE TOPIC	FUNCTIONS	LISTENING AND SPEAKING	VOCABULARY	GRAMMAR FOCUS
Unit 6 **Time** pages 70–81 **Topic:** Daily activities and time	• Describing habitual activities • Asking for dates and times • Giving information about dates and times	• Using *usually* vs. *always* • Using *has* vs. *goes to* for classes	• Times of day • Habitual activities	• Simple present tense • *Wh-* questions • Prepositions of time (*at, in, on*)
Review: Units 5 and 6 pages 82–83		• Understanding a conversation		
Unit 7 **Shopping** pages 84–95 **Topic:** Food and money	• Asking about quantity • Reading prices • Asking the location of items	• Asking and answering *How many?* and *How much?*	• Grocery store items • U.S. currency	• Count and non-count nouns • *How many? / How much?* • *There is / There are* • Quantifiers with non-count nouns
Unit 8 **Work** pages 96–107 **Topic:** Jobs and skills	• Identifying past and present jobs • Describing work and life skills	• Talking about your job • Talking about job skills	• Occupations • Work locations	• Simple past of *be* (statements and questions) • *Can* • Contractions
Review: Units 7 and 8 pages 108–109		• Understanding a narrative		
Unit 9 **Daily living** pages 110–121 **Topic:** Home responsibilities	• Describing past actions • Discussing chores • Expressing appreciation	• Talking about household activities	• Chores • Household items • Time words	• Simple past tense of regular and irregular verbs
Unit 10 **Leisure** pages 122–133 **Topic:** Free time	• Describing past actions • Describing future actions • Discussing plans	• Talking about leisure activities	• Leisure activities • Sports	• Simple past tense of irregular verbs • Future with *be going to*
Review: Units 9 and 10 pages 134–135		• Understanding a conversation		

Projects pages 136–140
Self-assessments pages 141–145
Reference pages 146–154
    Grammar charts pages 146–150
    Useful lists pages 151–153
    Map of North America page 154
Self-study audio script pages 155–159

READING	WRITING	LIFE SKILLS	PRONUNCIATION
• Reading a paragraph describing a person's schedule • Using *Wh-* questions to interpret a reading	• Writing a description of your schedule • Using indents for paragraphs	• Using class and other schedules • Understanding Parent-Teacher Associations • Understanding volunteerism • Using calendars • Understanding holidays • Reading clocks	• Pronouncing key vocabulary
			• Understanding intonation in questions
• Reading a paragraph describing a shopping trip • Looking for clues to understand new words	• Writing a note about a shopping list • Using commas in a list	• Reading supermarket ads • Reading receipts and using basic consumer math • Understanding the food pyramid • Using U.S. currency • Using multiple payment methods	• Pronouncing monetary values
• Reading a letter describing a person's job and work history • Interpreting narrative time through verb tense	• Writing a paragraph about your life and work skills • Checking spelling	• Completing job applications • Identifying work and life skills • Understanding job certification • Reading e-mail	• Pronouncing key vocabulary
			• Pronouncing the *-s* ending with plural nouns
• Reading a letter describing daily events • Interpreting the narrative voice	• Writing a letter describing household chores • Using the past tense in writing	• Using a job-duties chart • Understanding household chores and tools used for them • Reading clothing-care labels	• Pronouncing key vocabulary
• Reading a letter describing a vacation • Interpreting time words in a passage	• Writing a letter describing a family's weekend activities • Creating new paragraphs as the tense changes	• Reading a TV schedule • Using schedules • Understanding the cultural features of sports	• Pronouncing key vocabulary
			• Pronouncing the *-ed* ending in the simple past

To the teacher

What is Ventures?

Ventures is a five-level, standards-based, integrated-skills series for adult students. The five levels, which are Basic through Level Four, are for low-beginning literacy to high-intermediate students.

The *Ventures* series is flexible enough to be used in open enrollment, managed enrollment, and traditional programs. Its multilevel features support teachers who work with multilevel classes.

What components does *Ventures* have?

Student's Book with Self-study Audio CD

Each **Student's Book** contains a Welcome Unit and ten topic-focused units, plus five review units, one after every two units. Each unit has six skill-focused lessons. Projects, self-assessments, and a reference section are included at the back of the Student's Book.

- **Lessons** are self-contained, allowing for completion within a one-hour class period.
- **Review lessons** recycle, reinforce, and consolidate the materials presented in the previous two units and include a pronunciation activity.
- **Projects** offer community-building opportunities for students to work together, using the Internet or completing a task, such as making a poster or a book.
- **Self-assessments** are an important part of students' learning and success. They give students an opportunity to evaluate and reflect on their learning as well as a tool to support learner persistence.
- The **Self-study Audio CD** is included at the back of the Student's Book. The material on the CD is indicated in the Student's Book by an icon SELF-STUDY AUDIO CD.

Teacher's Edition with Teacher's Toolkit Audio CD/CD-ROM

The interleaved **Teacher's Edition** walks instructors step-by-step through the stages of a lesson.

- Included are learner-persistence and community-building tasks as well as teaching tips, expansion activities, and ways to expand a lesson to two or three instructional hours.

- The Student's Book answer key is included on the interleaved pages in the Teacher's Edition.
- The Teacher's Toolkit Audio CD/CD-ROM contains additional reproducible material for teacher support. Included are picture dictionary cards and worksheets, tests with audio, and student self-assessments for portfolio assessment. Reproducible sheets also include cooperative learning activities. These activities reinforce the materials presented in the Student's Book and develop social skills, including those identified by SCANS[1] as being highly valued by employers.
- The unit, midterm, and final tests are found on both the Teacher's Toolkit Audio CD/CD-ROM and in the Teacher's Edition. The tests include listening, vocabulary, grammar, reading, and writing sections.

Audio Program

The *Ventures* series includes the *Class Audio* and the *Student Self-study Audio* SELF-STUDY AUDIO CD. The Class Audio contains all the listening materials in the Student's Book and is available on CD or audiocassette. The Student Self-study Audio CD contains all the unit conversations, readings, and picture dictionary words from the Student's Book.

Workbook

The **Workbook** has two pages of activities for each lesson in the Student's Book.

- The exercises are designed so learners can complete them in class or independently. Students can check their own answers with the answer key in the back of the Workbook. Workbook exercises can be assigned in class, for homework, or as student support when a class is missed.
- Grammar charts at the back of the Workbook allow students to use the Workbook for self-study.
- If used in class, the Workbook can extend classroom instructional time by 30 minutes per lesson.

Add Ventures

Add Ventures is a book of reproducible worksheets designed for use in multilevel classrooms. The worksheets give students 15–30 minutes additional practice with each lesson and can be used with homogeneous or heterogeneous groupings. These

---

[1] The Secretary's Commission on Achieving Necessary Skills, which produced a document that identifies skills for success in the workplace. For more information, see wdr.doleta.gov/SCANS.

worksheets can also be used as targeted homework practice at the level of individual students, ensuring learner success.

There are three tiered worksheets for each lesson.

- **Tier 1 Worksheets** provide additional practice for those who are at a level slightly below the Student's Book or who require more controlled practice.
- **Tier 2 Worksheets** provide additional practice for those who are on the level of the Student's Book.
- **Tier 3 Worksheets** provide additional practice that gradually expands beyond the text. These multilevel worksheets are all keyed to the same answers for ease of classroom management.

Unit organization

Within each unit there are six lessons:

LESSON A Get ready The opening lesson focuses students on the topic of the unit. The initial exercise, *Talk about the picture*, involves one "big" picture. The visuals create student interest in the topic and activate prior knowledge. They help the teacher assess what learners already know and serve as a prompt for the key vocabulary of each unit. Next is *Listening*, which is based on short conversations. The accompanying exercises give learners the opportunity to relate vocabulary to meaning and to relate the spoken and written forms of new theme-related vocabulary. The lesson concludes with an opportunity for students to practice language related to the theme in a communicative activity, either orally with a partner or individually in a writing activity.

LESSONS B and C focus on grammar. The sections move from a *Grammar focus* that presents the grammar point in chart form; to *Practice* exercises that check comprehension of the grammar point and provide guided practice; and, finally, to *Communicate* exercises that guide learners as they generate original answers and conversations. The sections on these pages are sometimes accompanied by a *Culture note*, which provides information directly related to the conversation practice (such as the use of titles with last names), or a *Useful language* note, which provides several expressions that can be used interchangeably to accomplish a specific language function (such as greetings).

LESSON D Reading develops reading skills and expands vocabulary. The lesson opens with a *Before you read* exercise, whose purpose is to activate prior knowledge and encourage learners to make predictions. A *Reading tip*, which focuses learners on a specific reading skill, accompanies the **Read** exercise. The reading section of the lesson concludes with **After you read** exercises that check students' understanding. In the Basic Student's Book and Student's Books 1 and 2, the vocabulary expansion portion of the lesson is a **Picture dictionary**. It includes a *word bank*, pictures to identify, and a conversation for practicing the new words. The words are intended to expand vocabulary related to the unit topic. In Student's Books 3 and 4, the vocabulary expansion portion of the lesson occurs in **Check your understanding**.

LESSON E Writing provides writing practice within the context of the unit. There are three kinds of exercises in the lesson: prewriting, writing, and postwriting. **Before you write** exercises provide warm-up activities to activate the language students will need for the writing and one or more exercises that provide a model for students to follow when they write. A *Writing tip*, which presents information about punctuation or organization directly related to the writing assignment, accompanies the **Write** exercise. The Write exercise sets goals for the student writing. In the **After you write** exercise, students share with a partner using guided questions and the steps of the writing process.

LESSON F Another view has three sections.

- **Life-skills reading** develops the scanning and skimming skills that are used with documents such as forms, charts, schedules, announcements, and ads. Multiple-choice questions that follow the document develop test-taking skills similar to CASAS[2] and BEST.[3] This section concludes with an exercise that encourages student communication by providing questions that focus on some aspect of information in the document.
- **Fun with language** provides exercises that review and sometimes expand the topic, vocabulary, or grammar of the unit. They are interactive activities for partner or group work.
- **Wrap up** refers students to the self-assessment page in the back of the book, where they can check their knowledge and evaluate their progress.

The Author Team

Gretchen Bitterlin   Sylvia Ramirez
Dennis Johnson   K. Lynn Savage
Donna Price

[2] The Comprehensive Adult Student Assessment System. For more information, see www.casas.org.
[3] The Basic English Skills Test. For more information, see www.cal.org/BEST.

Correlations

UNIT/PAGES	CASAS	EFF
Unit 1 **Personal information** pages 6–17	0.1.2, 0.1.3, 0.1.4, 0.1.5, 0.1.6, 0.2.1, 0.2.2, 2.1.1, 2.1.8, 2.4.1, 2.5.5, 2.7.2, 4.8.1, 6.0.1, 7.2.4, 7.4.3, 7.5.6	Most EFF Standards are met, with particular focus on: • Conveying ideas in writing • Listening actively • Practicing lifelong learning skills • Reading with understanding • Seeking feedback and revising accordingly • Speaking so others can understand • Testing learning in real-life applications • Understanding and working with numbers
Unit 2 **At school** pages 18–29	0.1.2, 0.1.4, 0.1.5, 2.5.5, 4.5.3, 4.6.2, 4.6.5, 4.7.2, 4.7.4, 4.8.1, 6.0.1, 6.0.2, 6.1.1, 7.1.4, 7.4.5	Most EFF Standards are met, with particular focus on: • Assessing the needs of others • Attending to visual sources of information • Interacting with others in positive ways • Offering input • Organizing and presenting information • Seeking feedback and revising accordingly • Understanding and working with numbers
Unit 3 **Friends and family** pages 32–43	0.1.2, 0.1.4, 0.2.1, 0.2.4, 1.4.1, 2.6.1, 2.7.1, 2.7.2, 6.0.1, 6.0.2, 7.1.4, 7.2.4, 7.4.7, 7.4.8, 7.5.6, 8.1.3, 8.2.1, 8.3.1	Most EFF Standards are met, with particular focus on: • Cooperating with others • Listening actively • Making inferences, predictions, or judgments • Monitoring comprehension • Organizing and relaying information effectively • Paying attention to the conventions of the English language • Seeking feedback and revising accordingly
Unit 4 **Health** pages 44–55	0.1.1, 0.1.2, 0.1.3, 0.1.4, 0.2.1, 0.2.3, 2.1.8, 2.3.2, 2.5.3, 2.5.5, 3.1.1, 3.1.2, 3.1.3, 3.2.1, 3.2.3, 3.3.1, 3.4.1, 3.4.3, 3.5.7, 4.6.1, 4.8.1, 6.0.1, 7.2.2, 7.2.4, 7.2.6, 7.3.2, 7.5.5, 7.5.6	Most EFF Standards are met, with particular focus on: • Anticipating and identifying problems • Attending to oral communication • Defining what one is trying to achieve • Gathering facts and supporting information • Organizing and relaying spoken information effectively • Selecting appropriate reading strategies • Taking responsibility for learning
Unit 5 **Around town** pages 58–69	0.1.1, 0.1.2, 0.1.3, 0.1.4, 0.2.1, 0.2.3, 1.1.3, 1.3.7, 1.4.1, 1.9.2, 1.9.4, 2.2.1, 2.2.3, 2.2.5, 2.5.4, 2.6.3, 4.8.1, 5.2.4, 6.0.1, 6.6.5, 7.1.2, 7.1.4, 7.2.2, 7.2.4, 7.2.7, 7.3.2, 7.3.4, 7.4.8, 7.5.6, 8.3.2	Most EFF Standards are met, with particular focus on: • Assessing interests, resources, and the potential for success • Attending to visual sources of information • Defining what one is trying to achieve • Establishing goals based on one's own current and future needs • Identifying and using strategies appropriate to goals and tasks • Organizing and relaying spoken information effectively • Understanding, interpreting, and working with symbolic information

SCANS	BEST Plus Form A	BEST Form B
Most SCANS standards are met, with particular focus on: • Acquiring and evaluating information • Improving basic language skills • Interpreting and communicating information • Organizing and maintaining information • Working with diversity	Overall test preparation is supported, with particular impact on the following items: Locator: W1–W7 Level 1: 2.2, 2.3 Level 2: 4.1 Level 3: 5.1	Overall test preparation is supported, with particular impact on the following areas: • Directions/Clarification • Envelopes • Greetings • Housing • Oral interview • Personal background forms • Telephone directories • Time/Numbers
Most SCANS standards are met, with particular focus on: • Acquiring and evaluating information • Allocating material and facility resources • Knowing how to learn • Monitoring and correcting performance • Participating as a member of a team • Solving problems	Overall test preparation is supported, with particular impact on the following items: Level 2: 4.1, 4.2, 5.1, 5.2	Overall test preparation is supported, with particular impact on the following areas: • Calendar • Employment • Oral interview • Personal information • Reading passages • Writing notes
Most SCANS standards are met, with particular focus on: • Interpreting and communicating information • Knowing how to learn • Participating as a member of a team • Practicing self-management • Understanding social systems	Overall test preparation is supported, with particular impact on the following items: Locator: W1–W7 Level 1: 2.1, 2.2, 2.3, 4.1, 4.2, 4.3 Level 2: 1.2, 1.3, 4.2 Level 3: 1.3, 4.1, 4.2	Overall test preparation is supported, with particular impact on the following areas: • Home environment • Oral interview • Personal information • Reading signs, ads, and notices • Time
Most SCANS standards are met, with particular focus on: • Acquiring and evaluating information • Improving basic skills • Interpreting and communicating information • Organizing and maintaining information • Practicing reasoning • Working with diversity	Overall test preparation is supported, with particular impact on the following items: Level 2: 4.2 Level 3: 1.2	Overall test preparation is supported, with particular impact on the following areas: • Accidents • Doctor/Health • Oral interview • Personal information • Telephone directory
Most SCANS standards are met, with particular focus on: • Interpreting and communicating information • Organizing and maintaining information • Solving problems • Understanding systems • Working with diversity	Overall test preparation is supported, with particular impact on the following items: Locator: W2, W6, W8 Level 1: 1.3, 2.3, 3.1, 3.2, 3.3, 4.1, 4.2, 4.3 Level 2: 2.1, 3.1, 4.1, 5.2 Level 3: 4.1, 4.2, 5.1	Overall test preparation is supported, with particular impact on the following areas: • Directions • Oral interview • Personal information • Reading passages

UNIT/PAGES	CASAS	EFF
Unit 6 **Time** pages 70–81	0.1.2, 0.1.4, 0.2.4, 2.3.1, 2.3.2, 2.5.5, 2.6.1, 2.6.3, 2.7.1, 4.1.6, 4.1.7, 4.2.1, 4.3.1, 6.0.1, 6.0.3, 7.1.2, 7.1.4, 7.2.4, 8.1.1, 8.1.2, 8.1.3	Most EFF Standards are met, with particular focus on: • Attending to visual sources of information • Communicating using a variety of mathematical representations • Paying attention to the conventions of spoken English • Setting and prioritizing goals • Understanding, interpreting, and working with numbers and symbolic information
Unit 7 **Shopping** pages 84–95	0.1.2, 0.2.4, 1.1.6, 1.1.7, 1.2.1, 1.2.2, 1.2.5, 1.3.1, 1.3.6, 1.3.8, 1.5.1, 1.5.3, 1.6.4, 1.8.1, 1.8.2, 2.6.4, 6.0.1, 6.0.2, 6.0.3, 6.0.4, 6.1.1, 6.1.2, 6.2.1, 6.2.2, 6.2.5, 6.5.1, 6.6.7, 6.9.2, 7.1.3, 7.1.4, 7.2.3, 7.5.6, 8.2.1	Most EFF Standards are met, with particular focus on: • Cooperating with others • Determining the reading purpose • Integrating information with prior knowledge • Monitoring the effectiveness of communication • Seeking feedback and revising accordingly • Speaking so others can understand • Using math to solve problems and communicate
Unit 8 **Work** pages 96–107	0.1.2, 0.2.1, 0.2.2, 1.9.6, 4.1.1, 4.1.2, 4.1.5, 4.1.6, 4.1.8, 4.4.2, 4.4.4, 4.4.7, 4.5.1, 4.6.2, 7.1.1, 7.1.4, 7.2.3, 7.2.4, 7.5.1, 7.5.6, 8.2.1, 8.2.6	Most EFF Standards are met, with particular focus on: • Conveying ideas in writing • Cooperating with others • Listening actively • Speaking so others can understand • Taking stock of where one is
Unit 9 **Daily living** pages 110–121	0.1.2, 0.2.4, 1.4.1, 1.7.4, 2.3.2, 4.6.3, 7.1.4, 7.2.2, 7.4.8, 7.5.1, 7.5.5, 8.1.1, 8.1.4, 8.2.1, 8.2.2, 8.2.3, 8.2.4, 8.2.5, 8.2.6, 8.3.1	Most EFF Standards are met, with particular focus on: • Attending to visual sources of information • Cooperating with others • Integrating readings with prior knowledge • Monitoring the effectiveness of communication • Organizing and presenting written information • Setting and prioritizing goals
Unit 10 **Leisure** pages 122–133	0.1.2, 0.1.4, 0.2.4, 2.3.2, 2.6.1, 2.6.2, 2.6.3, 5.2.4, 6.0.1, 6.0.3, 7.1.4, 7.5.1, 7.5.6	Most EFF Standards are met, with particular focus on: • Determining the communication purpose • Interacting with others in positive ways • Monitoring listening comprehension • Reflecting and evaluating • Seeking feedback and revising accordingly • Speaking so others can understand

SCANS	BEST Plus Form A	BEST Form B
Most SCANS standards are met, with particular focus on: • Allocating time • Interpreting and communicating information • Organizing and maintaining information • Participating as a member of a team • Practicing reasoning • Seeing things in the mind's eye	Overall test preparation is supported, with particular impact on the following items: Locator: W5–W7 Level 1: 3.3, 4.1, 4.2, 4.3 Level 2: 2.2, 4.2 Level 3: 4.1, 4.2, 5.2	Overall test preparation is supported, with particular impact on the following areas: • Oral interview • Personal information • Reading passages • Reading signs, ads, and notices • Time
Most SCANS standards are met, with particular focus on: • Allocating money • Organizing and maintaining information • Participating as a member of a team • Practicing arithmetic and mathematics • Understanding social and organizational systems	Overall test preparation is supported, with particular impact on the following items: Level 1: 1.2, 1.3, 3.3 Level 2: 3.1, 3.2, 3.3 Level 3: 1.1, 1.2, 1.3	Overall test preparation is supported, with particular impact on the following areas: • Checks • Food labels • Oral interview • Reading signs, ads, and notices • Shopping and money
Most SCANS standards are met, with particular focus on: • Assessing knowledge and skills • Interpreting and communicating information • Knowing how to learn • Participating as a member of a team • Practicing self-management	Overall test preparation is supported, with particular impact on the following items: Locator: W1–W7 Level 2: 1.2 Level 3: 2.3	Overall test preparation is supported, with particular impact on the following areas: • Calendar • Employment • Oral interview • Personal information form
Most SCANS standards are met, with particular focus on: • Allocating time • Improving basic skills • Interpreting and communicating information • Seeing things in the mind's eye • Working with diversity	Overall test preparation is supported, with particular impact on the following items: Locator: W6 Level 1: 2.3 Level 2: 1.2, 1.3	Overall test preparation is supported, with particular impact on the following areas: • Home environment • Oral interview • Personal information • Reading passages • Reading signs, ads, and notices
Most SCANS standards are met, with particular focus on: • Interpreting and communicating information • Participating as a member of a team • Practicing reasoning • Practicing self-management • Seeing things in the mind's eye	Overall test preparation is supported, with particular impact on the following items: Locator: W6 Level 1: 4.1, 4.2, 4.3 Level 3: 4.1, 4.2	Overall test preparation is supported, with particular impact on the following areas: • Notes • Oral interview • Personal information • Reading passages • Reading signs, ads, and notices • Shopping and money

Meet the Ventures author team

Gretchen Bitterlin has been an ESL instructor and ESL department instructional leader with the Continuing Education Program, San Diego Community College District. She now coordinates that agency's large noncredit ESL program. She was also an ESL Teacher Institute Trainer and Chair of the TESOL Task Force on Adult Education Program Standards. She is a co-author of *English for Adult Competency*.

Dennis Johnson has been an ESL instructor at City College of San Francisco, teaching all levels of ESL, since 1977. As ESL Site Coordinator, he has provided guidance to faculty in selecting textbooks. He is the author of *Get Up and Go* and co-author of *The Immigrant Experience*.

Donna Price is Associate Professor of ESL and Vocational ESL/Technology Resource Instructor for the Continuing Education Program, San Diego Community College District. She has taught all levels of ESL for 20 years and is a former recipient of the TESOL Newbury House Award for Excellence in Teaching. She is also the author of *Skills for Success*.

Sylvia Ramirez is a professor at Mira Costa College, where she coordinates the large noncredit ESL program. She has more than 30 years of experience in adult ESL, including multilevel ESL, vocational ESL, family literacy, and distance learning. She has represented the California State Department of Education in providing technical assistance to local ESL programs.

K. Lynn Savage, Series Editor, is a retired ESL teacher and Vocational ESL Resource teacher from City College of San Francisco, who trains teachers for adult education programs around the country. She chaired the committee that developed *ESL Model Standards for Adult Education Programs* (California, 1992) and is the author, co-author, and editor of many ESL materials including *Teacher Training through Video, Parenting for Academic Success: A Curriculum for Families Learning English, Crossroads Café, Building Life Skills, Picture Stories, May I Help You?,* and *English That Works*.

To the student

Welcome to the *Ventures* series! We want you to enjoy using your *Ventures* Student's Book in your classroom. We also hope that you will use this book to study on your own. For that reason, the Student's Book comes with an audio CD. Use it at home to review and practice the material you are learning in class. You will make faster progress in learning English if you take the time to study at home and do your homework.

Good luck in your studies!

The Author Team
Gretchen Bitterlin
Dennis Johnson
Donna Price
Sylvia Ramirez
K. Lynn Savage

Welcome

1 Meet your classmates

Look at the picture. What do you see?

Library hours

Mon.-Wed.
9 a.m.-9 p.m.
Thurs.-Sat.
9 a.m.-6 p.m.

September

Sun	Mon	Tue	Wed	Thurs	Fri	Sat
						1
2	3	4	5	6	7	8
9	10	11	12	13	14	15
16	17	18	19	20	21	22
23	24	25	26	27	28	29
30						

Return books here.

English classes start Monday, September 17

C-D

A-B

2 The alphabet

A Listen and repeat.

Aa	Bb	Cc	Dd	Ee	Ff	Gg	Hh	Ii
Jj	Kk	Ll	Mm	Nn	Oo	Pp	Qq	Rr
Ss	Tt	Uu	Vv	Ww	Xx	Yy	Zz	

B **Write** the letters.

CAPITAL LETTERS

A _A_	B ___	C ___	D ___	E ___	F ___	G ___	H ___	I ___	J ___
K ___	L ___	M ___	N ___	O ___	P ___	Q ___	R ___	S ___	T ___
U ___	V ___	W ___	X ___	Y ___	Z ___				

lowercase letters

a _a_	b ___	c ___	d ___	e ___	f ___	g ___	h ___	i ___	j ___
k ___	l ___	m ___	n ___	o ___	p ___	q ___	r ___	s ___	t ___
u ___	v ___	w ___	x ___	y ___	z ___				

Talk with a partner. Take turns. Say a letter.
Your partner points to the letter.

SELF-STUDY AUDIO CD

C Listen and repeat.

A What's your name?
B Helena.
A How do you spell that?
B H-E-L-E-N-A.

Talk to five classmates. Write the names.

Class list

Helena

1.

2.

3.

4.

5.

3 Numbers

SELF-STUDY AUDIO CD

A 🎧 **Listen and repeat.**

0 zero	1 one	2 two	3 three	4 four	5 five
6 six	7 seven	8 eight	9 nine	10 ten	
11 eleven	12 twelve	13 thirteen	14 fourteen	15 fifteen	
16 sixteen	17 seventeen	18 eighteen	19 nineteen	20 twenty	

Talk with a partner. Take turns. Say a number. Your partner points to the number.

SELF-STUDY AUDIO CD

B 🎧 **Listen.** Circle the number you hear.

1. **0** (**6**) **16**   4. **2**   **5**   **15**   7. **8**   **9**   **10**
2. **3**   **7**   **20**   5. **1**   **9**   **17**   8. **3**   **5**   **13**
3. **1**   **10**   **11**   6. **11**   **12**   **20**   9. **14**   **15**   **16**

SELF-STUDY AUDIO CD

C 🎧 **Listen.** Write the number you hear.

1. _3_   3. ____   5. ____   7. ____   9. ____
2. ____   4. ____   6. ____   8. ____   10. ____

D **Write.** Match the number and the word.

| 1 | 2 | 3 | 4 | 5 | 6 | 7 | 8 | 9 | 10 |

| three | five | four | two | one | nine | six | ten | eight | seven |

Talk with a partner. Take turns. Spell a number. Your partner says the number.

n-i-n-e

9

4 Days and months

A 🔊 **Listen and repeat.**

Sunday	Monday	Tuesday	Wednesday	Thursday	Friday	Saturday

Talk with a partner. Take turns. Say a day. Your partner points to the day.

B Write the full spelling.

1. Sun. _____Sunday_____   5. Thurs. _____

2. Mon. _____   6. Fri. _____

3. Tues. _____   7. Sat. _____

4. Wed. _____

C 🔊 **Listen and repeat.**

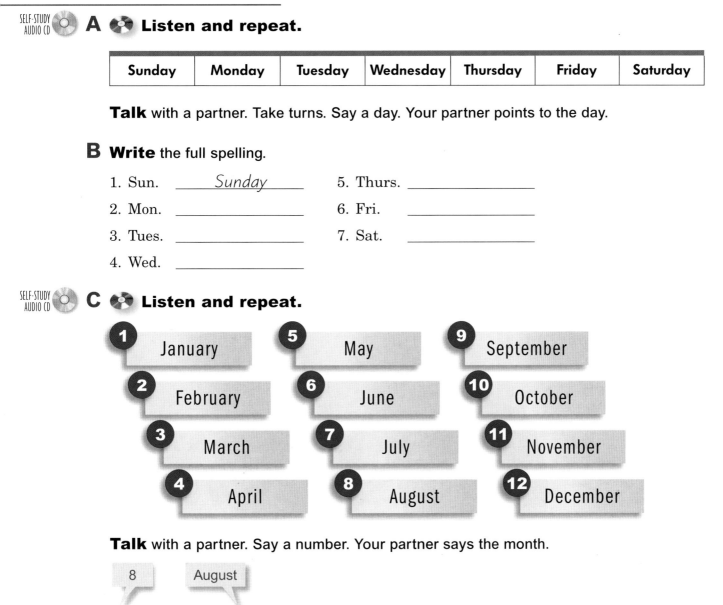

1	January	5	May	9	September
2	February	6	June	10	October
3	March	7	July	11	November
4	April	8	August	12	December

Talk with a partner. Say a number. Your partner says the month.

8   August

D Talk with a partner. Tell the month of the holiday.

1. Thanksgiving
2. Halloween
3. New Year's Day
4. Labor Day
5. Mother's Day
6. Father's Day

Thanksgiving

November

Lesson A Get ready

1 Talk about the picture

A Look at the picture. What do you see?

B Point to: first name • last name • city
zip code • area code • telephone number

REGISTRATION OFFICE

REGISTRATION HOURS
6 p.m. – 9 p.m.

LAST NAMES
A–G

LAST NAMES
H–P

LAST NAMES
Q–Z

COLLEGE

September

COURSE SCHEDULE

SUBJECT	TEACHER'S NAME	ROOM NUMBER
Intro to Computers	Mrs. Dieguez	365
Beginning ESL	Ms. Nelson	119
Intermediate ESL	Mr. Black	247
Advanced ESL	Ms. Weaver	210
Business English	Mr. Novak	322
Business Math	Mrs. Johnson	324
Citizenship	Ms. Franco	108
GED	Mr. Horn	135

COURSE GUIDE

RICARDO

MR. CLARK

REGISTRATION FORM

Name	Svetlana Kulik
Phone	(707) 555-9073
Address	1041 Main Street Napa, California 94558

2 Listening

SELF-STUDY
AUDIO CD

A 🎧 **Listen.** Circle the words you hear.

address	country	middle name
area code	first name	(telephone number)
city	last name	zip code

SELF-STUDY
AUDIO CD

B 🎧 **Listen again.** Write the letter of the conversation.

1. _____

MR. CLARK

2. _____

RICARDO

3. _____

Mike
213-555-8907
Suzie
213-709-

4. _____

Ricardo Juan Perez
350 Lincoln Avenue
Napa, California 94558

5. _____

REGISTRATION FORM
Name   Svetlana Kulik
Phone   (707) 555-9073
Address 1041 Main Street
         Napa, California 94558

6. _a_

21 555-8907

Listen again. Check your answers.

C **Write.** Complete the sentences about yourself.

1. My first name is _____ .

2. My last name is _____ .

3. My area code is _____ .

4. My telephone number is _____ .

Talk with a partner. Talk about yourself.

My first name is Dahlia.   My first name is Yuri.

Saying telephone numbers
Stop at each number. Say *oh* for *zero*.

5   5   5   -   2   0   1   6
five - five - five   two - oh - one - six

What's your name?

1 Grammar focus: possessive adjectives

Questions				Answers	
What's	your	name?		My	name is Svetlana.
What's	his	name?		His	name is Steve.
What's	her	name?		Her	name is Mary.
What are	their	names?		Their	names are Ted and Rob.

What's = What is

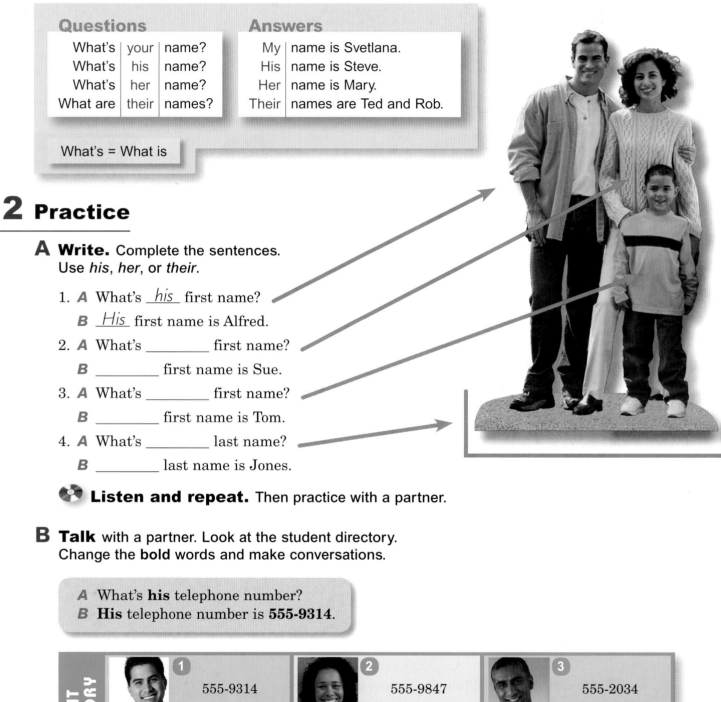

2 Practice

A Write. Complete the sentences.
Use *his*, *her*, or *their*.

1. **A** What's _his_ first name?
   B _His_ first name is Alfred.
2. **A** What's _____ first name?
   B _____ first name is Sue.
3. **A** What's _____ first name?
   B _____ first name is Tom.
4. **A** What's _____ last name?
   B _____ last name is Jones.

Listen and repeat. Then practice with a partner.

B Talk with a partner. Look at the student directory.
Change the **bold** words and make conversations.

A What's **his** telephone number?
B **His** telephone number is **555-9314**.

STUDENT DIRECTORY

1 555-9314	**2** 555-9847	**3** 555-2034
4 555-5093	**5** 555-6172	**6** 555-8216

C 🔊 **Listen.** Then listen and repeat.

> **A** What's your name?
> **B** **Jennifer Kent.**
> **A** Sorry. What's your first name?
> **B** My first name is **Jennifer**.
> **A** How do you spell that?
> **B** **J-E-N-N-I-F-E-R.**
> **A** OK. What's your last name?
> **B** **Kent. K-E-N-T.**

Useful language

Please spell that.
*How do you spell **Jennifer**?*

Talk in groups. Ask questions and write the names.

First name	Last name
Jennifer	Kent

3 Communicate

A **Talk** with your classmates. Introduce a classmate.

> This is my new classmate. Her first name is Jennifer. Her last name is Kent.

B **Talk** with a partner. Take turns and make new conversations.

> **A** Good morning.
> **B** Good morning.
> **A** My name is Anna Gray.
>   What's your name?
> **B** Kate Harris.
> **A** Nice to meet you.
> **B** Nice to meet you, too.

> **A** Hi. My name is Peter.
> **B** Hi. My name is Alan.
> **A** Nice to meet you, Alan.
> **B** Nice to meet you, too, Peter.

Culture note

Some people have two first names:
Mei-Hwa

Some people have two last names:
Baker-Price

Are you from Canada?

1 Grammar focus: subject pronouns; simple present of *be*

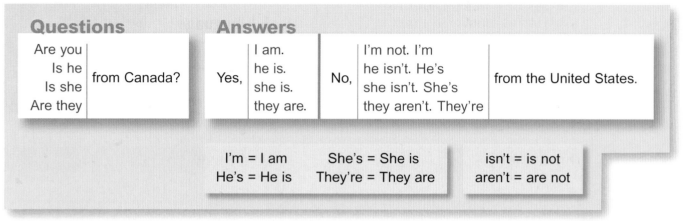

Questions		Answers			
Are you Is he Is she Are they	from Canada?	Yes,	I am. he is. she is. they are.	No,	I'm not. I'm he isn't. He's she isn't. She's they aren't. They're	from the United States.

I'm = I am	She's = She is	isn't = is not
He's = He is	They're = They are	aren't = are not

2 Practice

A Write. Complete the sentences.

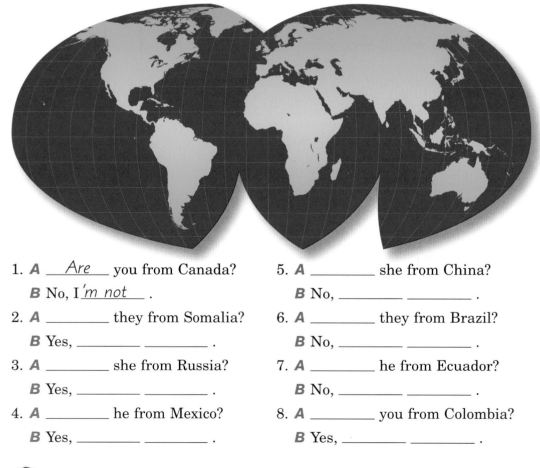

1. **A** ___Are___ you from Canada?
   B No, I _'m not_ .

2. **A** _____ they from Somalia?
   B Yes, _____ _____ .

3. **A** _____ she from Russia?
   B Yes, _____ _____ .

4. **A** _____ he from Mexico?
   B Yes, _____ _____ .

5. **A** _____ she from China?
   B No, _____ _____ .

6. **A** _____ they from Brazil?
   B No, _____ _____ .

7. **A** _____ he from Ecuador?
   B No, _____ _____ .

8. **A** _____ you from Colombia?
   B Yes, _____ _____ .

Listen and repeat. Then practice with a partner.

B Talk with a partner. Change the **bold** words and make conversations.

INTERNATIONAL FESTIVAL

A Is he from **Mexico**?
B Yes, **he is**.

A Are they from **the United States**?
B No, **they aren't. They're** from **India**.

1. Japan? 2. the United States? 3. Mexico? 4. India? 5. Mexico? 6. Japan?

C 💿 Listen and repeat. Then practice with a partner.

A Where are you from, **Katia**?
B I'm from **Brazil**.
A Brazil? How do you spell that?
B B-R-A-Z-I-L.

Useful language
Where are you from?
Where do you come from?

3 Communicate

Talk in groups. Where are your classmates from? Make guesses.

A This is Katia. Where is she from?
B Is she from Colombia?
A No, she isn't.
B Is she from Brazil?
A Yes, she is.

Lesson D *Reading*

1 Before you read

Talk. Svetlana starts school today. Look at the registration form. Answer the questions.

1. What's her last name?
2. What's her telephone number?

2 Read

SELF-STUDY
AUDIO CD **Listen and read.**

REGISTRATION FORM

Name	Svetlana Kulik
Phone	(707) 555-9073
Address	1041 Main Street Napa, California 94558

A New Student

Svetlana Kulik is a new student. She is from Russia. Now she lives in Napa, California. Her address is 1041 Main Street. Her zip code is 94558. Her area code is 707. Her telephone number is 555-9073.

Addresses with 3 numbers
832 Main Street
eight thirty-two

Addresses with 4 numbers
1041 Main Street
ten forty-one

3 After you read

A Read the sentences. Are they correct? Circle *Yes* or *No*.

1. Svetlana is a new teacher.	Yes	(No)
2. Her last name is Kulik.	Yes	No
3. She is from Colombia.	Yes	No
4. Her address is 1014 Main Street.	Yes	No
5. Her zip code is 94558.	Yes	No
6. Her area code is 555-9073.	Yes	No

Write. Correct the sentences.

1. Svetlana is a new <u>student</u>.

B Write. Answer the questions about Svetlana.

1. What is her last name? _____
2. Is she from Russia? _____
3. What is her address? _____
4. What is her telephone number? _____

Picture dictionary *Personal information*

1. _____title_____

2. _____

3. _____

4. _____

5. _____

6. _____

7. _____

8. _____

9. _____

Student ID

Mr. Rafael A. Gomez
263 Midlane Street
Apt. 3B
New York, NY 10012

Rafael A. Gomez

SELF-STUDY AUDIO CD

A **Write** the words in the picture dictionary. Then listen and repeat.

address	middle initial	street
apartment number	signature	title
city	state	zip code

Culture note
Use *Mr.* for a man.
Use *Ms.* for a woman.
Use *Mrs.* for a married woman.
Use *Miss* for an unmarried woman.

B **Talk** with a partner. Ask and answer questions.
Complete the student ID with your partner's information.

STUDENT ID

What's your name?

My name is Rafael.

Lesson E *Writing*

1 Before you write

A Talk with your classmates. Ask questions. Write the answers.

> **A** What's your name?
> **B** My name is **Liliana Lopez**.
> **A** What's your telephone number?
> **B** My telephone number is **555-2904**.
> **A** Where are you from?
> **B** I'm from **Mexico**.

Begin names of people, streets, cities, states, and countries with capital letters.
These are capital letters: *A B C D E*
These are lowercase letters: *a b c d e*

Name	Telephone number	Country
Liliana Lopez	555-2904	Mexico

B Write. Complete the sentences. Use the words in the box.

> address   last name   zip code
> area code   telephone number

Svetlana is a new student.

1. Her _____last name_____ is Kulik. She is from Russia.
2. Her _____ is 1041 Main Street.
3. Her _____ is 94558.
4. Her _____ is 555-9073.
5. Her _____ is 707.

C Write. Add capital letters.

Student News

P
~~p~~edro is a new student. He is from colombia. His last name is ramirez. His address is 285 pacheco street, houston, texas. His zip code is 77057. His telephone number is 555-7878. His area code is 713.

D Read about Pedro again. Complete the chart. Use capital letters.

First name	Last name	City	State
Pedro			

2 Write

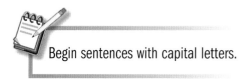

Begin sentences with capital letters.

Read the questions and write about yourself.

1. What's your first name? _My first name is_ _____.
2. What's your last name? _____
3. What's your address? _____
4. What's your zip code? _____
5. What's your telephone number? _____
6. Where are you from? _____

3 After you write

A Read your sentences to a partner.

B Check your partner's sentences.
- What is your partner's name?
- Are the capital letters correct?

1 Life-skills reading

Registration

Please print.

☐ Mr.   ☐ Ms.   ☐ Mrs.

(1) NAME: _____
                Last   First   Middle

(2) ADDRESS: _____
              Number   Street   Apt.

(3) _____
              City   State   Zip code

(4) TELEPHONE: _____
              Area code   Number

(5) COUNTRY OF ORIGIN: _____

(6) _____
              Signature

A **Read** the questions. Look at the form. Circle the answers.

1. Where do you print your country of origin?
   a. line 1
   b. line 2
   c. line 5
   d. line 6

2. Where do you print your name?
   a. line 1
   b. line 3
   c. line 5
   d. line 6

3. Where do you sign your name?
   a. line 1
   b. line 3
   c. line 5
   d. line 6

4. Where do you write your zip code?
   a. line 2
   b. line 3
   c. line 4
   d. line 5

B **Write.** Complete the form with your own information.

C **Talk** in groups. Look at your forms. Ask and answer questions.

What's your last name?   My last name is Hom.

2 Fun with language

A Talk about names with your classmates.

1. Who do you call by a first name?
2. Who do you call by a title and last name?
3. Who do you call by other names?

B Talk. Read the conversation. Then introduce two classmates to each other.

Mr. Jones, this is my friend Tony. Tony, this is my teacher Mr. Jones.

Nice to meet you, Tony.

Nice to meet you, too, Mr. Jones.

C Work in a group. Write your last names. Then write your names again in alphabetical order.

Last name	Alphabetical order

Alphabetical order is *A – B – C* order.
Alvarez
Baker
Chang

3 Wrap up

Complete the **Self-assessment** on page 141.

1 Talk about the picture

A Look at the picture. What do you see?

B Point to: a book • a desk • a map • a pencil
a clock • an eraser • a pen • a table

At school

Lesson
Review: name, address, phone number
New: school vocabulary
Book: Ventures, pages 18–19

Ventures

Mr. Liang

DICTIONARY
DICTIONARY

2 Listening

SELF-STUDY
AUDIO CD **A** 👁️ **Listen.** Circle the words you hear.

book	eraser	notebook	(pens)
calculator	map	pencils	rulers

SELF-STUDY
AUDIO CD **B** 👁️ **Listen again.** Write the letter of the conversation.

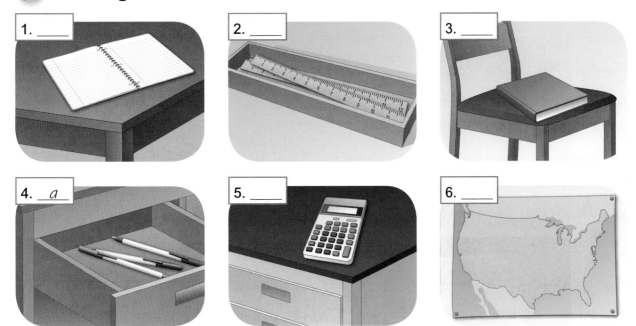

1. _____ 2. _____ 3. _____

4. _a_ 5. _____ 6. _____

Listen again. Check your answers.

C Write. What's on the desk? What's on the table?

book	clock	eraser	notebook	pencil	ruler

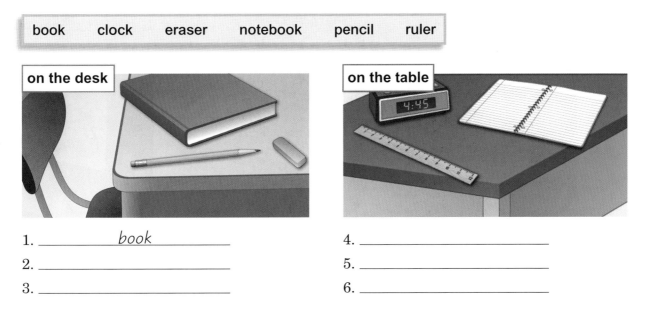

on the desk

on the table

1. _____book_____   4. _____

2. _____   5. _____

3. _____   6. _____

Where is the pen?

1 Grammar focus: prepositions *in* and *on; Where is?*

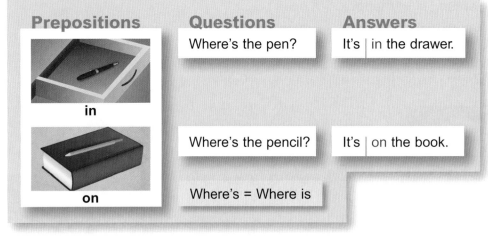

Prepositions	Questions	Answers
in	Where's the pen?	It's | in the drawer.
on	Where's the pencil?	It's | on the book.
	Where's = Where is	

2 Practice

A Write. Complete the sentences. Use *in* or *on*.

1

A Where's the book?
B It's __on__ the shelf.

2

A Where's the pencil sharpener?
B It's _____ the wall.

3

A Where's the dictionary?
B It's _____ the table.

4

A Where's the calendar?
B It's _____ the box.

5

A Where's the eraser?
B It's _____ the drawer.

6

A Where's the calculator?
B It's _____ the cabinet.

🔊 **Listen and repeat.** Then practice with a partner.

B Listen. Circle the items you hear.

Talk with a partner. Look at the picture again. Change the **bold** words and make conversations.

> **A** Excuse me. Where's the **calculator**?
> **B** It's **in the cabinet**.
> **A** Oh, thanks.
> **B** You're welcome.

> **Useful language**
> Say *excuse me* to get someone's attention.

3 Communicate

Talk with a partner about your classroom.

> Where's the computer?   It's on the table.

Lesson C *Where are the pencils?*

1 Grammar focus: singular and plural nouns

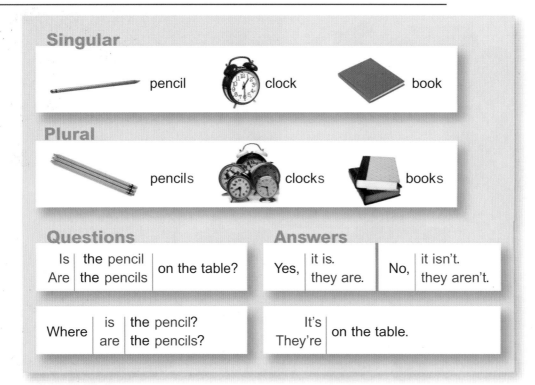

Singular

—— pencil   clock   book

Plural

pencils   clocks   books

Questions

Is	the pencil	on the table?
Are	the pencils	

Where	is	the pencil?
	are	the pencils?

Answers

Yes,	it is.	No,	it isn't.
	they are.		they aren't.

It's	on the table.
They're	

2 Practice

A Write. Look at the picture. Complete the conversations.

1. **A** Are the _____*books*_____ in the cabinet?
                     (book / books)

   B Yes, _____*they are*_____ .

2. **A** Is the _____ in the cabinet?
                 (clock / clocks)

   B Yes, _____ .

3. **A** Are the _____ on the table?
                 (ruler / rulers)

   B No, _____ .

4. **A** Are the _____ on the table?
                 (pencil / pencils)

   B No, _____ .

5. **A** Are the _____ on the table?
              (calculator / calculators)

   B Yes, _____ .

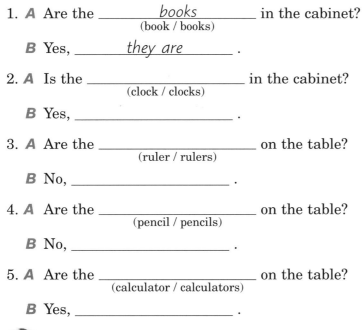

🔊 **Listen and repeat.** Then practice with a partner.

B Write. Complete the sentences. Use *is* or *are*.

1. Where __*is*__ the computer?   4. Where _____ the maps?

2. Where _____ the notebooks?   5. Where _____ the pencils?

3. Where _____ the calendar?   6. Where _____ the calculator?

C Write. Look at the picture. Read the answers. Write the questions.

1. **A** *Where are the pencils* ?   4. **A** _____ ?

   B They're on the desk.   **B** It's on the desk.

2. **A** _____ ?   5. **A** _____ ?

   B It's on the filing cabinet.   **B** They're in the filing cabinet.

3. **A** _____ ?   6. **A** _____ ?

   B It's on the wall.   **B** They're in the box.

Listen and repeat. Then practice with a partner.

3 Communicate

Talk with a partner about things in your classroom.

> **A** Is the map on the desk?
> **B** Yes, it is.
> **A** Are the books on the table?
> **B** No, they aren't.
> **A** Where are they?
> **B** They're in the cabinet.

Lesson D *Reading*

1 Before you read

Talk. It's the first day of class. Look at the picture. Answer the questions.

1. What do you see in the classroom?
2. Where are the objects?

2 Read

SELF-STUDY AUDIO CD

Listen and read.

Attention, new students!

Welcome to your new classroom.

• The computer is on the small table.
• The pencils are in the basket on the desk.
• The erasers are in the basket.
• The books are in the bookcase.
• The calculators are on the bookcase.
• The markers are in the desk drawer.

Look at pictures before you read. They help you understand new words. *Basket* is a new word. Find the basket in the picture.

3 After you read

A Read the sentences. Are they correct? Circle *Yes* or *No*.

1. The computer is on the desk.	Yes	(No)
2. The pencils are in the basket.	Yes	No
3. The erasers are in the bookcase.	Yes	No
4. The books are in the bookcase.	Yes	No
5. The calculators are in the bookcase.	Yes	No
6. The markers are in the desk drawer.	Yes	No

Write. Correct the sentences.

1. The computer is on the <u>small table</u>.

B Write. Answer the questions about the classroom.

1. Where is the desk? _____
2. Where is the basket? _____

Picture dictionary *Classroom objects*

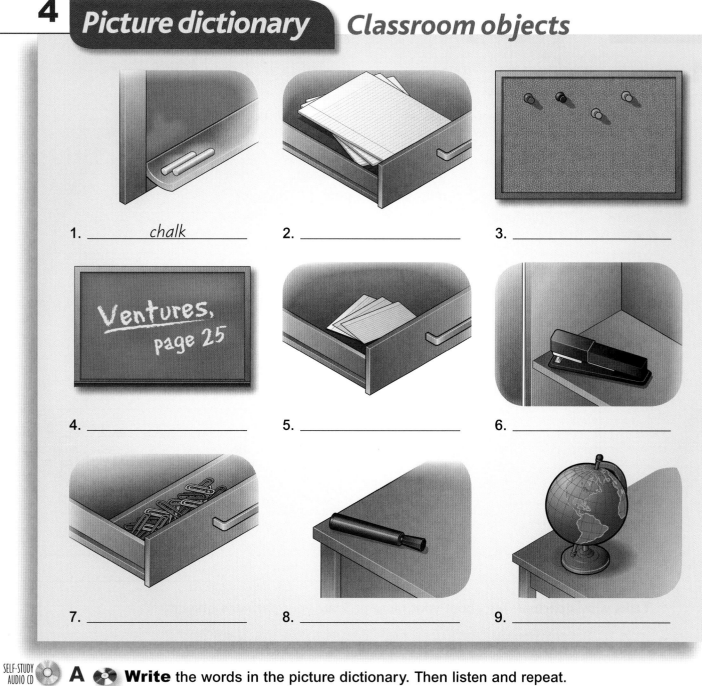

1. _____chalk_____
2. _____
3. _____
4. _____
5. _____
6. _____
7. _____
8. _____
9. _____

SELF-STUDY AUDIO CD

A 💿 **Write** the words in the picture dictionary. Then listen and repeat.

bulletin board	chalkboard	index cards	notepads	stapler
chalk	globe	marker	paper clips	

B Talk with a partner. Look at the pictures and make conversations.

A Where's the chalk?
B It's on the chalk tray.
A Where are the paper clips?
B They're in the drawer.

1 Before you write

A Draw. Choose six objects. Draw two on the desk. Draw two on the table. Draw two in the cabinet. Write the words under the picture.

calculator	clock	globe	notepad	pencil sharpener
calendar	computer	map	pen	ruler
chalk	dictionary	notebook	pencil	stapler

_____   _____   _____

_____   _____   _____

Talk with a partner. Tell about your picture. Draw your partner's objects.

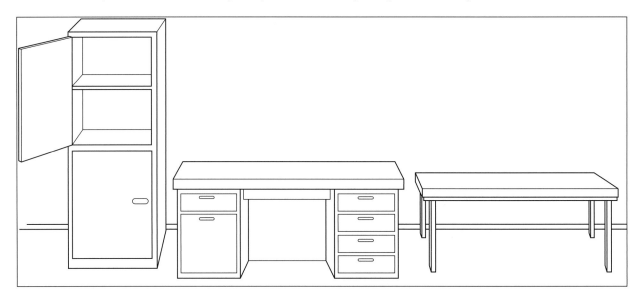

B **Write.** Look at the picture. Complete the sentences. Use *is* or *are* with *on* or *in*.

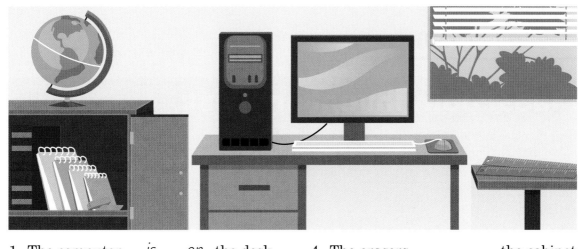

1. The computer __is__ __on__ the desk.
2. The notepads _____ ____ the cabinet.
3. The book _____ ____ the cabinet.
4. The erasers _____ ____ the cabinet.
5. The globe _____ ____ the cabinet.
6. The rulers _____ ____ the table.

2 Write

Write. Look at your classroom. What do you see? Complete the chart.

Singular	Plural
pen	pencils

Write one sentence about each object.

1. _The pen is on the desk._
2. _The pencils are in the drawer._
3. _____
4. _____
5. _____
6. _____

> Start sentences with a capital letter (A, B, C). End sentences with a period (.).

3 After you write

A **Read** your sentences to a partner.

B **Check** your partner's sentences.
- What are four objects in the classroom? Where are they?
- Are the capital letters and periods correct?

Another view

1 Life-skills reading

Classroom Inventory List

Item		Number	Location
calculators		15	in the drawer
computers		1	on the desk
books		5	on the cabinet
erasers		20	in the box
pencils		20	on the table
pens		20	on the table
rulers		25	in the cabinet

A **Read** the questions. Look at the inventory list. Circle the answers.

1. How many rulers are in the cabinet?
   a. 5
   b. 15
   c. 20
   d. 25

2. What's on the desk?
   a. a pen
   b. a book
   c. a computer
   d. a calculator

3. Where are the calculators?
   a. in the cabinet
   b. in the drawer
   c. on the desk
   d. on the table

4. Where are the books?
   a. on the desk
   b. on the cabinet
   c. in the drawer
   d. in the cabinet

B **Talk** with a partner. Ask and answer questions about the inventory list.

Are the pens on the table?

Yes, they are.

Where are the books?

They're on the cabinet.

2 Fun with language

A **Work with a partner.** Complete the words. Are the objects in your classroom?

	Yes	No		Yes	No
pe _n_ s	☑	☐	penc ___ ls	☐	☐
___ rasers	☐	☐	___ ap	☐	☐
c ___ alk	☐	☐	___ uler ___	☐	☐
no ___ ebo ___ ks	☐	☐	___ alend ___ r	☐	☐
gl ___ be	☐	☐	___ tap ___ er	☐	☐

Write the missing letters from the chart.

_n_ __ __ __ __ __ __ __ __ __ __ __ __ __

Write. Unscramble the letters to answer the question.

Where are you?   ___ _n_ ___ ___ ___   ___ ___ ___ ___ ___ ___ ___ ___

B **Work in a group.** Make a classroom inventory list.

Classroom Inventory List

Item	Number	Location
erasers	3	on the shelf

Talk. Tell your class about your inventory.

> Three erasers are on the shelf.

3 Wrap up

Complete the **Self-assessment** on page 141.

Review

1 Listening

Read the questions. Then listen and circle the answers.

1. What is Juan's last name?   (a.) Perez   b. Cruz
2. Where is he from?   a. Mexico   b. El Salvador
3. What is his apartment number?   a. 1324   b. 10
4. What is his zip code?   a. 94548   b. 94321
5. What is his area code?   a. 213   b. 555
6. What is his telephone number?   a. 555-6301   b. 555-0133

Talk with a partner. Ask and answer the questions. Use complete sentences.

2 Grammar

A Write. Complete the story.

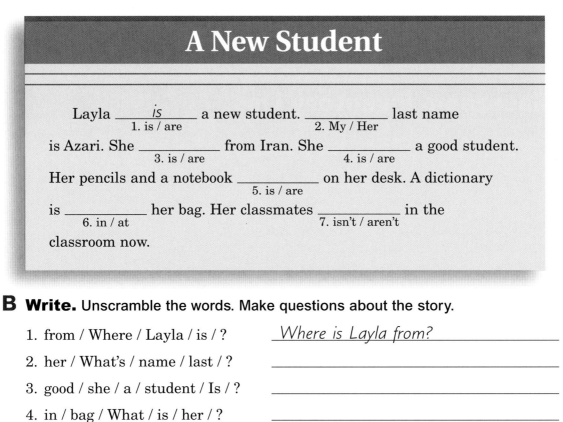

A New Student

Layla ____is____ a new student. _____ last name
    1. is / are   2. My / Her

is Azari. She _____ from Iran. She _____ a good student.
            3. is / are   4. is / are

Her pencils and a notebook _____ on her desk. A dictionary
                           5. is / are

is _____ her bag. Her classmates _____ in the
    6. in / at   7. isn't / aren't

classroom now.

B Write. Unscramble the words. Make questions about the story.

1. from / Where / Layla / is / ?   _Where is Layla from?_
2. her / What's / name / last / ?   _____
3. good / she / a / student / Is / ?   _____
4. in / bag / What / is / her / ?   _____

Talk with a partner. Ask and answer the questions.

3 Pronunciation: syllables

A 🔘 **Listen** to the syllables in these words.

•   • •   • • •

name   address   apartment

B 🔘 **Listen and repeat.** Say the word and clap one time for each syllable.

•	• •	• • •
map	classroom	initial
books	middle	telephone
box	partner	signature
clock	chalkboard	computer
pens	ruler	sharpener
chair	notebook	cabinet
desk	pencil	eraser

Talk with a partner. Take turns. Say a word. Your partner claps for each syllable.

C 🔘 **Listen** to the words. Write the number of syllables you hear.

a. __1__   c. ____   e. ____   g. ____

b. ____   d. ____   f. ____   h. ____

🔘 **Listen again** and repeat. Clap one time for each syllable.

D **Write.** Find 10 other words in your book. Make a list.

1.	6.
2.	7.
3.	8.
4.	9.
5.	10.

Talk with a partner. Say the words. Your partner says how many syllables.

Lesson A Get ready

1 Talk about the picture

A Look at the picture. What do you see?

B Point to: the mother • the father • the daughter
the son • the grandmother • the grandfather

2 Listening

SELF-STUDY
AUDIO CD

A **Listen.** Circle the words you hear.

brother	grandfather	mother
daughter	(grandmother)	sister
father	husband	son

SELF-STUDY
AUDIO CD

B **Listen again.** Write the letter of the conversation.

1. ____   2. ____   3. ____   4. _a_   5. ____   6. ____

Listen again. Check your answers.

C **Write.** Who lives with you? Check (✓) your answers.

☐ my husband   ☐ my son   ☐ my mother   ☐ my sister
☐ my wife   ☐ my daughter ☐ my father   ☐ my brother

Talk about your family. Work in a group.

My husband and my son live with me.
My mother and father live in Ecuador.

What are you doing?

1 Grammar focus: present continuous; *Wh-* questions

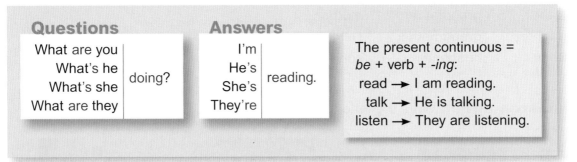

Questions		Answers		The present continuous = *be* + verb + *-ing*:
What are you	doing?	I'm	reading.	read ➝ I am reading.
What's he		He's		talk ➝ He is talking.
What's she		She's		listen ➝ They are listening.
What are they		They're		

2 Practice

A Write. Complete the conversations.

A What's she doing?
B _She's reading_____ .
       (read)

A What's he doing?
B _____ .
          (sleep)

A What are they doing?
B _____ .
          (eat)

A What's he doing?
B _____ TV.
         (watch)

A What's she doing?
B _____ .
          (talk)

A What are you doing?
B _____ .
          (study)

 Listen and repeat. Then practice with a partner.

B Talk with a partner. Point to the picture. Change the **bold** words and make conversations.

> **A** What**'s she** doing?
> **B** **She's listening to music.**

C Write. Answer the question.

What are you doing?

I'm _____ .

3 Communicate

Talk. Practice with a partner.

> **A** Hello?
> **B** Hi, Ann. This is Paul.
> **A** Oh, hi, Paul.
> **B** What are you doing?
> **A** I'm watching TV.
> **B** Well, today's my birthday.
>   I'm having my party now.
> **A** Now? Oh, no. I forgot!

Make new conversations.

Are you working now?

1 Grammar focus: present continuous; *Yes / No* questions

Questions		Answers			Spelling change
Are you			I am.		drive → driving
Is he	working?	Yes,	he is.	No,	take → taking
Is she			she is.		
Are they			they are.		

Answers — No:
I'm not.
he isn't.
she isn't.
they aren't.

2 Practice

A Write. Complete the conversations.

A Is she ___*working*___
(work)
now?

B Yes, she is. She's very busy.

A Is he _____
(drive)
to work?

B Yes, he is. He's late.

A Are they _____
(eat)
lunch now?

B Yes, they are. They're hungry.

A Is he _____
(help)
his grandmother?

B Yes, he is. He's really nice.

A Is she _____
(take)
a break?

B Yes, she is. She's tired.

A Are they _____
(buy)
water?

B Yes, they are. They're thirsty.

Listen and repeat. Then practice with a partner.

B Match. Complete the questions.

1. Is she working
2. Are you eating
3. Is he buying
4. Are they helping
5. Is he driving
6. Is she taking

a. lunch?
b. their grandmother?
c. to work?
d. a break?
e. a soda?
f. now?

C Look at the picture. Check (✓) *Yes* or *No*.

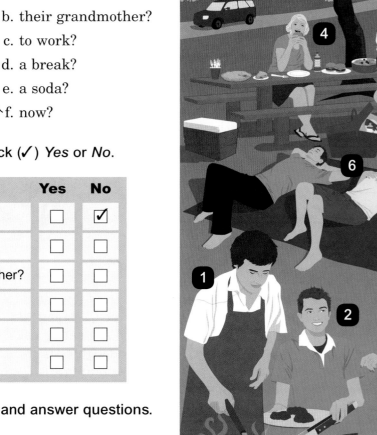

	Yes	No
1. Is he driving to work?	☐	✓
2. Is he helping his father?	☐	☐
3. Is she talking to her brother?	☐	☐
4. Is she eating lunch?	☐	☐
5. Is she working now?	☐	☐
6. Are they buying soda?	☐	☐

Talk with a partner. Ask and answer questions.

Is he driving to work?

No, he isn't. He's cooking lunch.

3 Communicate

Talk with a partner. Take turns. Act out and guess a word from the box.

tired	thirsty	hungry	busy

driving	studying	eating	working

Are you tired?

Yes, I am.

Are you working?

No, I'm not.

Lesson D Reading

1 Before you read

Talk. Juan is celebrating his 70th birthday. Look at the picture. Answer the questions.

1. What are the people doing?
2. Do you celebrate birthdays? How?

Photo Album

2 Read

SELF-STUDY AUDIO CD

Listen and read.

The Birthday Party

My name is Juan. In this picture, it's my birthday. I am 70 years old. Look at me! I don't look 70 years old. My wife, my daughter, and my grandson are eating cake. My grandson is always hungry. My granddaughter is drinking soda. She's always thirsty. My son-in-law is playing the guitar and singing. Everyone is happy!

Think about the title before you read. This helps you understand the story.

3 After you read

A Read the sentences. Are they correct? Circle *Yes* or *No*.

1. Juan is 17 years old.	Yes	(No)
2. Juan is celebrating his birthday with his friends.	Yes	No
3. His wife, daughter, and grandson are eating cake.	Yes	No
4. His granddaughter is drinking soda.	Yes	No
5. His grandson is playing the guitar and singing.	Yes	No
6. Everyone is tired.	Yes	No

Write. Correct the sentences.

1. Juan is 70 years old.

B Write. Answer the questions about Juan's birthday party.

1. What is Juan celebrating? _____
2. What is his family eating? _____
3. What is his granddaughter doing? _____
4. What is his son-in-law doing? _____

Picture dictionary *Family members*

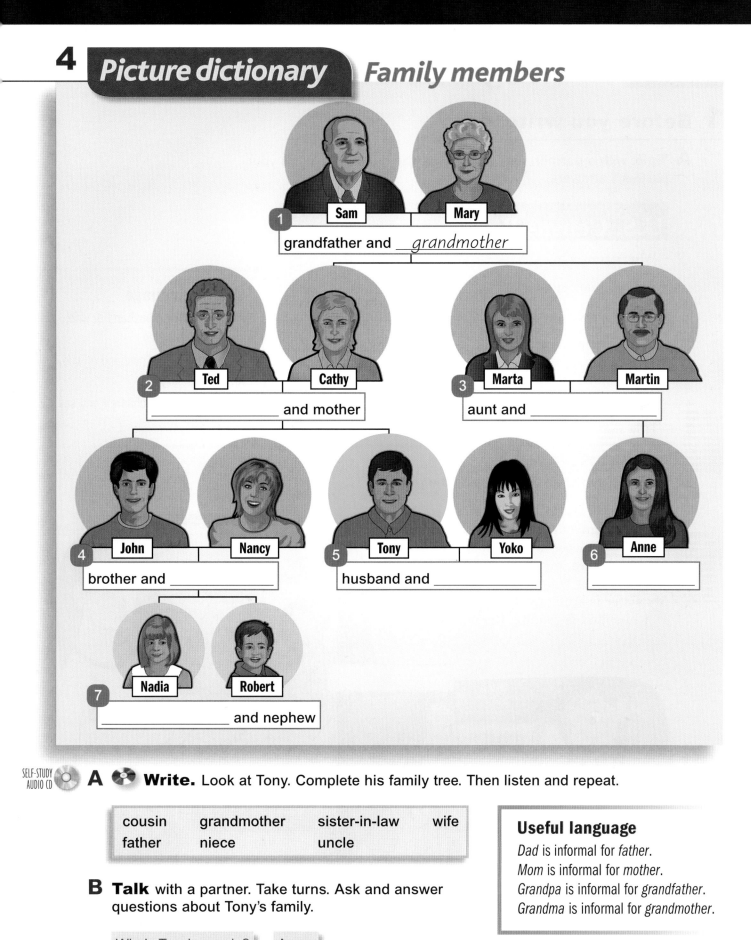

1. Sam — Mary
grandfather and *grandmother*

2. Ted — Cathy
_____ and mother

3. Marta — Martin
aunt and _____

4. John — Nancy
brother and _____

5. Tony — Yoko
husband and _____

6. Anne
_____

7. Nadia — Robert
_____ and nephew

SELF-STUDY
AUDIO CD

A **Write.** Look at Tony. Complete his family tree. Then listen and repeat.

cousin	grandmother	sister-in-law	wife
father	niece	uncle	

B **Talk** with a partner. Take turns. Ask and answer questions about Tony's family.

Who's Tony's cousin? Anne.

Useful language

Dad is informal for *father*.
Mom is informal for *mother*.
Grandpa is informal for *grandfather*.
Grandma is informal for *grandmother*.

Lesson E Writing

1 Before you write

A **Talk** with a partner. Ask and answer the questions. Write your partner's answers.

U.S. Census Bureau

What's your name? _____

Are you married or single? _____

Do you have children? _____

    How many daughters? _____

    How many sons? _____

How many sisters do you have? _____

How many brothers do you have? _____

Useful language

When you have a husband or wife, you say *I'm married*.

When you have no husband or wife, you say *I'm single*.

When you have no children, you say *I don't have any*.

B **Read.** Then write the words on the picture.

My name is David. I am single.
I live with my sister and her husband.
I have two nieces and one nephew.
In this picture, my nieces are <u>cooking</u>.
My nephew is <u>watching</u> TV.
My sister is <u>studying</u>. She's very smart.
Her husband is <u>reading</u> the newspaper.

cooking

2 Write

A Draw your family. What are they doing?

B Write about your picture. Answer the questions.

1. What's your name?

   My name is _____ .

2. Are you married or single?

   I'm _____ .

3. Who do you live with?

   I live with _____ .

4. How many are in your family?

   I have _____ .

5. In the picture, what are they doing?

   _____

   _____

   _____

> Spell numbers from one to ten:
> *I have* **one** *brother.*
> Write all other numbers:
> *I have* **11** *nieces.*

3 After you write

A Read your sentences to a partner.

B Check your partner's sentences.

- How many people are in the family?
- Did your partner spell the numbers from one to ten?

Another view

1 Life-skills reading

Insurance Application Form				
Last name	First name	Age	Male	Female
Parents				
Clark	Joseph	30	x	
Clark	Rita	29		x
Children				
Clark	Justin	10	x	
Clark	Scott	8	x	
Clark	Carolyn	7		x
Clark	Michael	2	x	

A Read the questions. Look at the form. Circle the answers.

1. How many children do Mr. and Mrs. Clark have?
   a. 1
   b. 2
   c. 3
   d. 4

2. How many daughters do Mr. and Mrs. Clark have?
   a. 1
   b. 2
   c. 3
   d. 4

3. How many sons do Mr. and Mrs. Clark have?
   a. 1
   b. 2
   c. 3
   d. 4

4. Who is eight years old?
   a. Carolyn
   b. Justin
   c. Michael
   d. Scott

B Talk in groups. Ask and answer questions about the Clark family.

How old is Michael?   He's two years old.

2 Fun with language

A Work with a partner. Read the sentences. Complete Jim's family tree.

1. Kate is Jim's wife.
2. Carol is Jim's sister.
3. Sarah is Jim's mother.
4. Burt is Jim's grandfather.
5. Rose is Jim's grandmother.
6. Bill is Jim's brother-in-law.
7. Todd is Jim's father.
8. Emily is Jim's daughter.
9. Chris is Jim's son.
10. Rob is Jim's nephew.

Useful language

Jim**'s** wife ➔ **his** wife
Carol**'s** son ➔ **her** son

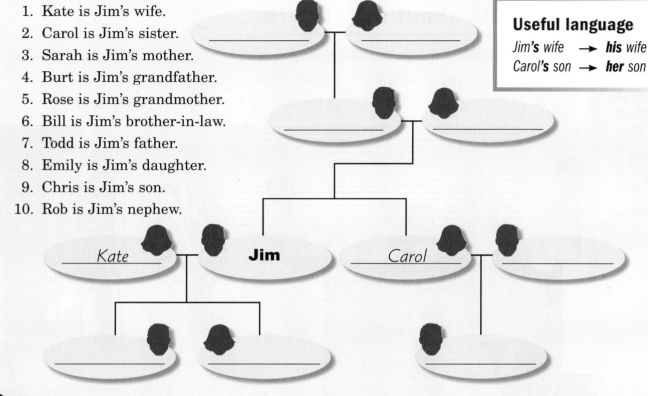

Kate   Jim   Carol

B Draw your family tree.

Talk with a partner. Show your family tree. Talk about your family.

3 Wrap up

Complete the **Self-assessment** on page 142.

Get ready

Health

1 Talk about the picture

A Look at the picture. What do you see?

B Point to a person with: a backache • a cough • a headache

a broken leg • an earache • a sore throat

Maria

2 Listening

SELF-STUDY AUDIO CD **A**  **Listen.** Circle the words you hear.

broken leg	earache	sore throat
cold	fever	sprained ankle
cough	(headache)	stomachache

SELF-STUDY AUDIO CD **B** **Listen again.** Write the letter of the conversation.

1. _____

2. _a_

3. _____

4. _____

5. _____

6. _____

Listen again. Check your answers.

C **Talk** with a partner. Take turns. Act out and guess the problem.

Sore throat?

Right.

Useful language
Yes.
Right.

I have a headache.

1 Grammar focus: simple present of *have*

Statements

I	have	
You	have	a cold.
He	has	
She	has	

Useful language

*I have a **terrible** cold.*
*I have a **bad** headache.*

2 Practice

A Write. Complete the sentences. Use *has* or *have*.

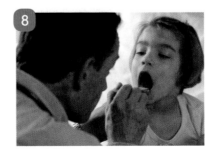

He _*has*_ a terrible cold.　　I _____ a headache.　　He _____ a backache.

You _____ a fever.　　I _____ a broken arm.　　He _____ a stomachache.

She _____ a bad cough.　　You _____ a sore throat.　　She _____ a cut.

🔊 **Listen and repeat.**

B 🔵 **Listen and repeat.** Then match.

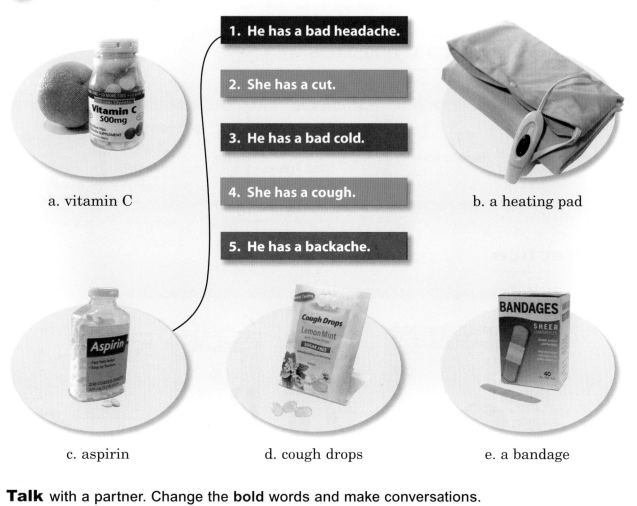

1. He has a bad headache.

2. She has a cut.

3. He has a bad cold.

4. She has a cough.

5. He has a backache.

a. vitamin C

b. a heating pad

c. aspirin

d. cough drops

e. a bandage

Talk with a partner. Change the **bold** words and make conversations.

A How **is he**?
B Not so good.
A What's wrong?
B **He has a bad headache.**
A I have **aspirin**.
B Really? Thanks.

Useful language
What's wrong?
What's the matter?

3 Communicate

Talk with a partner. Ask and answer questions.

A What's the matter?
B I have a cold.
A Take vitamin C.

Useful language
Take: *medicine, aspirin, vitamin C, cough drops*
Use: *a bandage, a heating pad*

Do you have a cold?

1 Grammar focus: questions with *have*

Questions		
Do	I	
Do	you	have a fever?
Does	he	
Does	she	

Answers				
	you	do.		
Yes,	I	do.		
	he	does.		
	she	does.		

	you	don't.
No,	I	don't.
	he	doesn't.
	she	doesn't.

don't = do not
doesn't = does not

2 Practice

A Write. Complete the sentences. Use *do*, *does*, *don't*, or *doesn't*.

1. Do I have a fever?
   No, you don't.

2. Does she have a sore throat?
   _____

3. Does he have a cough?
   _____

4. Do you have a cold?
   _____

5. Does she have the flu?
   _____

6. Does she have a sprained ankle?
   _____

Listen and repeat. Then practice with a partner.

B **Talk** with a partner. Change the **bold** words and make conversations.

> *A* **Mr. Jones** isn't at work today.
> *B* What's wrong with **him**? Does **he** have the flu?
> *A* No, **he doesn't**. **He** has a **backache**.

> *A* **Diana** isn't at work today.
> *B* What's wrong with **her**? Does **she** have the flu?
> *A* No, **she doesn't**. **She** has a **cold**.

Useful language

he → him
she → her

He is sick.
What's wrong with **him**?
She is sick.
What's wrong with **her**?

1. Mr. Jones

a backache

2. Diana

a cold

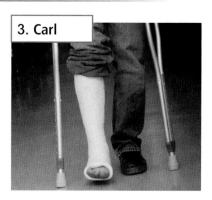
3. Carl

a broken leg

4. Mrs. Leeds

a stomachache

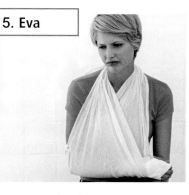
5. Eva

a broken arm

6. Ben

a fever

3 Communicate

Talk with a partner. Take turns and make conversations.

> *A* I don't feel well.
> *B* Do you have a cold?
> *A* No, I don't. I have a sore throat.
> *B* That's too bad. I hope you feel better.

Useful language

Get some rest.
I hope you feel better.

Lesson **D** *Reading*

1 Before you read

Talk. Maria is at the health clinic.
Look at the picture. Answer the questions.

1. Who is with Maria?
2. What's wrong?

2 Read

SELF-STUDY
AUDIO CD **Listen and read.**

The Health Clinic

Poor Maria! Everyone is sick! Maria and her
children are at the health clinic today. Her son, Luis,
has a sore throat. Her daughter, Rosa, has a
stomachache. Her baby, Gabriel, has an earache.
Maria doesn't have a sore throat. She doesn't
have a stomachache. And she doesn't have an
earache. But Maria has a very bad headache!

Look at the exclamation points (!) in
the reading. An exclamation point shows
strong feeling.

3 After you read

A Read the sentences. Are they correct? Circle *Yes* or *No*.

1. Maria and her children are at school.	Yes	No
2. Luis has a backache.	Yes	No
3. Rosa has a headache.	Yes	No
4. Gabriel has an earache.	Yes	No
5. Maria has a bad headache.	Yes	No
6. Everyone is happy today.	Yes	No

Write. Correct the sentences.

1. Maria and her children are at <u>the health clinic</u>.

B Write. Answer the questions about Maria.

1. Where are Maria and her three children today? _____

2. What's wrong with her baby? _____

3. What's the matter with Maria? _____

50   Unit 4

Picture dictionary   Parts of the body

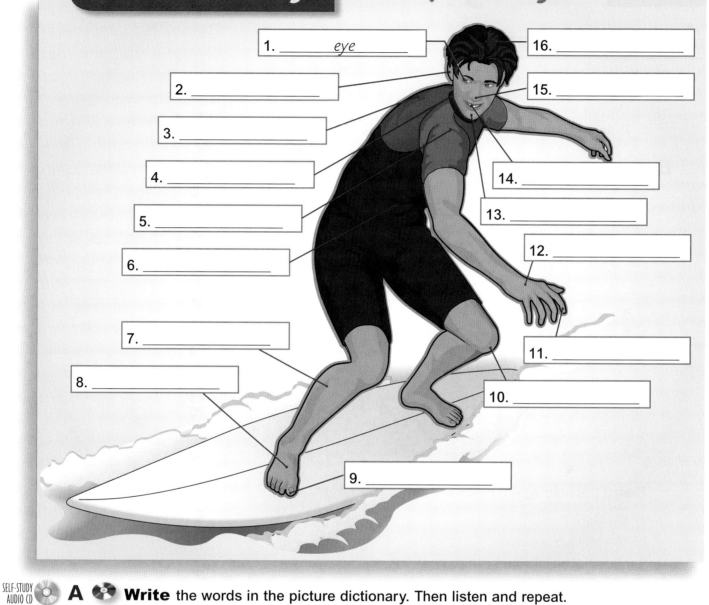

1. _____ *eye* _____

2. _____

3. _____

4. _____

5. _____

6. _____

7. _____

8. _____

9. _____

10. _____

11. _____

12. _____

13. _____

14. _____

15. _____

16. _____

SELF-STUDY AUDIO CD **A** 🔘 **Write** the words in the picture dictionary. Then listen and repeat.

back	ear	finger	hand	knee	neck	shoulder	toe
chin	eye	foot	head	leg	nose	stomach	tooth

B Talk with a partner. Change the **bold** word and make conversations.

> **A** What's wrong?
> **B** My **tooth** hurts.
> **A** That's too bad.

1 Before you write

A Talk with your classmates.

1. Do you write notes?
2. Who do you write to?

B Read. Luis is sick today. Read the note from his mother to his teacher.

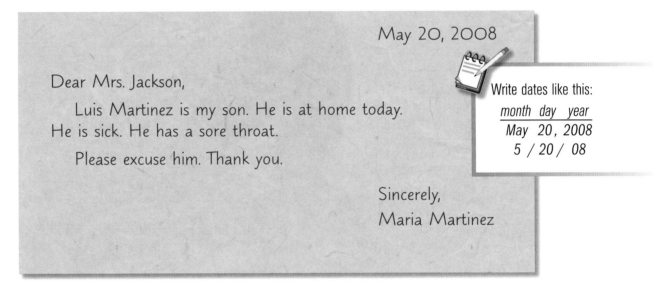

May 20, 2008

Dear Mrs. Jackson,

    Luis Martinez is my son. He is at home today.
He is sick. He has a sore throat.

    Please excuse him. Thank you.

Sincerely,
Maria Martinez

Write dates like this:
month day year
May 20, 2008
5 / 20 / 08

Read the note again. Circle the information.

1. the date
2. the teacher's name
3. the name of the sick child
4. what's wrong
5. the signature

Write. Answer the questions.

1. What is the date? _____

2. What is the teacher's name? _____

3. Who is sick? _____

4. What's the matter with him? _____

5. Who is the note from? _____

C **Write** about Rosa. She is sick, too. Complete the note.

| daughter | Dear | home | May 20, 2008 | stomachache |

May 20, 2008

_____ Mr. O'Hara,

    Rosa Martinez is my _____ . She is
at _____ today. She is sick. She has
a _____ .

    Please excuse her. Thank you.

                                        Sincerely,
                                        Maria Martinez

2 Write

Write. Imagine your son or daughter is sick today. Complete the note to the teacher.

                                        _____

Dear _____ ,
    _____ is my _____ .
    _____ is at home today. _____ is sick.
    _____ has a fever.
    Please excuse _____ . Thank you.
                                        Sincerely,

                                        _____

3 After you write

A **Read** your note to a partner.

B **Check** your partner's note.
  • Who is sick? What's the matter?
  • Is the date correct?

1 Life-skills reading

🩺 **Appointment Confirmation**

Here is your appointment information.

Patient: _____ J. D. Avona

Medical record number: _____ 9999999

Date: _____ Monday, October 23

Time: _____ 9:10 a.m.

Doctor: _____ William Goldman, MD

Address: _____ Eye Care Clinic

_____ 2025 Morse Avenue

Cancellation Information

To cancel only:	To cancel and reschedule:
(973) 555-5645	(973) 555-5210
7 days / 24 hours	Mon–Fri 8:30 a.m. to 5:00 p.m.

A Read the questions. Look at the appointment confirmation card. Circle the answers.

1. What is the doctor's last name?
   a. Avona
   b. Goldman
   c. Morse
   d. William

2. What is the appointment for?
   a. ears
   b. eyes
   c. nose
   d. throat

3. What is the address?
   a. Monday
   b. MD
   c. 2025 Morse Avenue
   d. 2025 Morris Avenue

4. What do you do to reschedule?
   a. call J. D. Avona
   b. call (973) 555-5645
   c. call (973) 555-5210
   d. go to the Eye Care Clinic

B Talk with your classmates. Ask and answer the questions.

1. Do you have a doctor?
2. Do you get appointment cards?
3. What information do your appointment cards have?

2 Fun with language

A Work in a group. Write the words in the webs.

aspirin	chin	finger	knee	sore throat	toothache
bandage	cough	heating pad	neck	stomachache	vitamin C

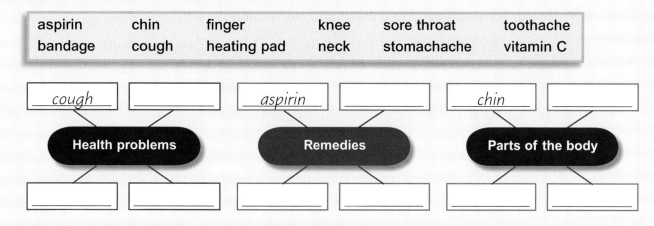

| _cough_ | | | _aspirin_ | | | _chin_ | |

Health problems   **Remedies**   **Parts of the body**

B Write. Look at the clues. Complete the puzzle.

Down ↓

Across →

Work with a partner. Check your answers.

3 Wrap up

Complete the **Self-assessment** on page 142.

Review

1 Listening

🔘 **Read** the questions. Then listen and circle the answers.

1. What's wrong with Connie?
   a. She has a backache.
   b. She has a headache.

2. What's wrong with Robert?
   a. He has an earache.
   b. He has a headache.

3. What's Robert doing?
   a. He's talking to the doctor.
   b. He's talking to the children.

4. What's Connie's daughter doing?
   a. She's sleeping.
   b. She's watching TV.

5. What's Connie's son doing?
   a. He's eating.
   b. He's watching TV.

6. What's wrong with Eddie?
   a. He has an earache.
   b. He has a stomachache.

Talk with a partner. Ask and answer the questions. Use complete sentences.

2 Grammar

A Write. Complete the story.

At the Hospital

This week, everyone in Anthony's family is sick. Anthony ____*has*____
                                                          1. have / has
a wife, a son, and a daughter. Right now, they _____ sitting in
                                                2. is / are
a hospital room. Anthony's wife _____ a backache. The nurse
                                 3. have / has
_____ giving her medicine. The doctor _____ talking to
4. is / are   5. is / are
Anthony. He _____ asking questions about the children. They
             6. is / are
_____ the flu.
7. have / has

B Write. Unscramble the words. Make questions about the story.

1. Is / home / family / at / Anthony's / ?   *Is Anthony's family at home?*

2. is / doing / the nurse / What / ? _____

3. wrong / the children / with / What's / ? _____

Talk with a partner. Ask and answer the questions.

3 Pronunciation: strong syllables

A 🔊 **Listen** to the syllables in these words.

•
happy

•
fever

B 🔊 **Listen and repeat.** Clap for each syllable. Clap loudly for the strong syllable.

•	• •	• • •	• • •
son	cooking	yesterday	tomorrow
wife	homework	grandmother	computer
head	toothache	grandfather	
ear	headache	newspaper	
foot	husband	studying	
leg	daughter	stomachache	

Talk with a partner. Take turns. Say each word. Your partner claps for each syllable.

C 🔊 **Listen** for the strong syllable in each word. Put a circle over the strong syllable.

1. father
2. earache
3. tired
4. birthday
5. thirsty
6. celebrate
7. finger
8. Brazil
9. repeat
10. elbow
11. reschedule
12. fever

D **Write** eight words from Units 3 and 4. Put a circle over the strong syllable in each word.

1.	5.
2.	6.
3.	7.
4.	8.

Talk with a partner. Read the names.

Lesson A *Get ready*

1 Talk about the picture

A Look at the picture. What do you see?

B Point to: a grocery store • a library • a restaurant
a hospital • a house • a street

2 Listening

SELF-STUDY
AUDIO CD **A** 🔘 **Listen.** Circle the words you hear.

bus stop	library	post office
(drugstore)	museum	restaurant
hospital	park	school

SELF-STUDY
AUDIO CD **B** 🔘 **Listen again.** Write the letter of the conversation.

1. _____

2. _____

3. _a_

4. _____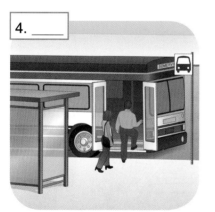

5. _____

6. _____

Listen again. Check your answers.

C Write. How many places are in your neighborhood?

museums _O_	libraries _____	schools _____
drugstores _____	restaurants _____	post offices _____
bus stops _____	parks _____	hospitals _____

Work with a partner. Ask and answer questions.

> How many museums are in your neighborhood?   None.

Useful language
When *0* means *not one*, say *none*.

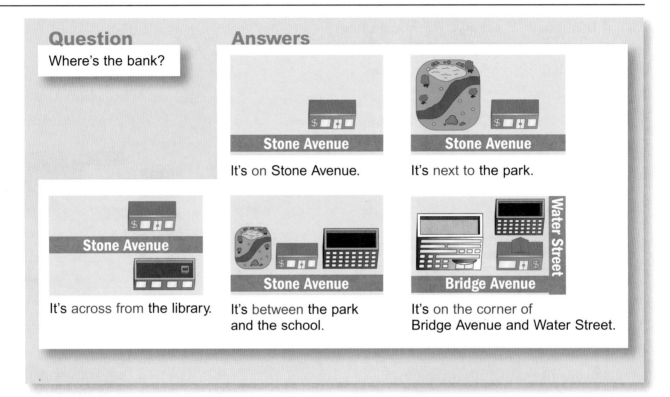

Lesson B *It's on the corner.*

1 Grammar focus: *on, next to, across from, between, on the corner of*

Question

Where's the bank?

Answers

It's on Stone Avenue.

It's next to the park.

It's across from the library.

It's between the park and the school.

It's on the corner of Bridge Avenue and Water Street.

2 Practice

A Write. Look at the map. Complete the sentences.

First Street

Grant Avenue

1. **A** Where's the park?

   B It's ___*next to*___ the bank.

2. **A** Where's the library?

   B It's _____ the bank.

3. **A** Where's the school?

   B It's _____ First Street and Grant Avenue.

4. **A** Where's the hospital?

   B It's _____ Grant Avenue.

5. **A** Where's the bank?

   B It's _____ the school and the park.

6. **A** Where's the post office?

   B It's _____ the library.

Listen and repeat. Then practice with a partner.

B 🔊 Listen and repeat.

> A Excuse me. Where's **Kim's Coffee Shop**?
> B It's **on Kent Street**.
> A Sorry. Could you repeat that, please?
> B It's **on Kent Street**.
> A Oh, OK. Thanks.

Useful language

Could you repeat that, please?
Sorry, I didn't get that.

Talk with a partner. Change the **bold** words and make conversations.

1 coffee shop

2 drugstore

3 grocery store

3 Communicate

A **Talk** with a partner. Look at the map on page 60. Give directions. Guess the place.

> A It's on the corner of First Street and Grant Avenue. It's across from the hospital.
> B The school?
> A That's right.

B **Draw** these places on the map. Talk with a partner. Ask and answer questions about your maps.

bank
bus stop
coffee shop
grocery store
hospital
house

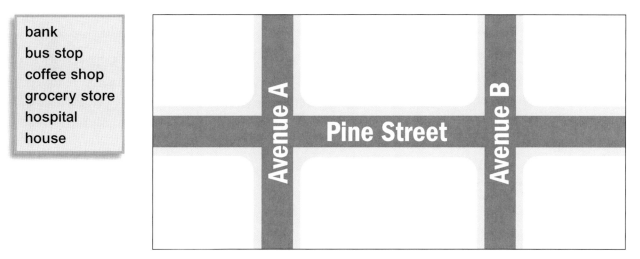

Go two blocks.

1 Grammar focus: imperatives

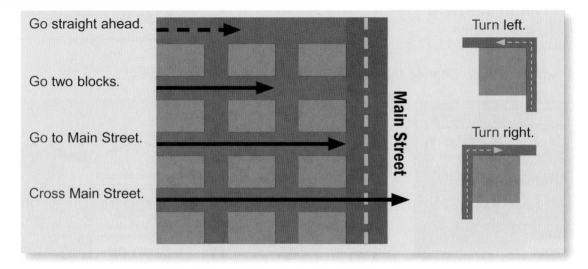

Go straight ahead.

Go two blocks.

Go to Main Street.

Cross Main Street.

Main Street

Turn left.

Turn right.

2 Practice

A Write. Match the pictures and the directions.

Cross Union Street.　　Go three blocks.　　Turn left.
Go straight ahead.　　Go to Main Street.　　Turn right.

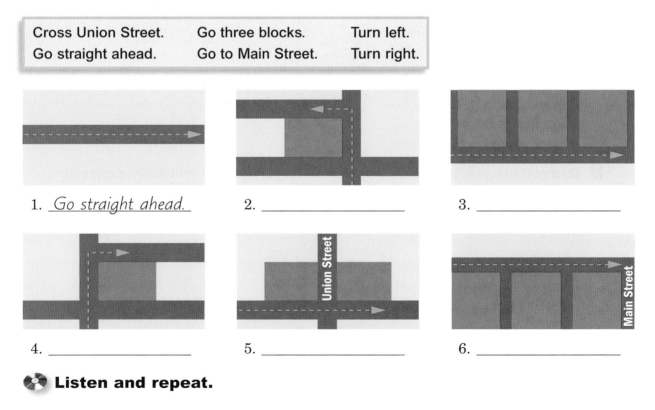

1. *Go straight ahead.*　　2. _____　　3. _____

4. _____　　5. _____　　6. _____

💿 **Listen and repeat.**

B Read the directions. Look at the map. Write the places.

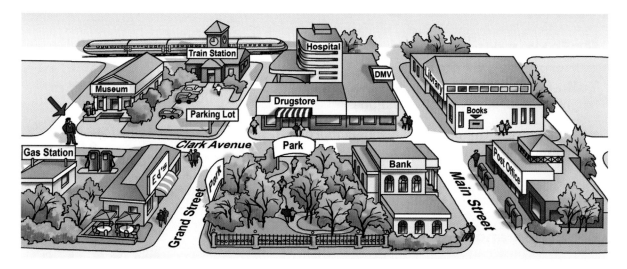

1. Go two blocks. Turn left. It's across from the library.

   the DMV

2. Go straight. Cross Grand Street. Turn right on Main Street. It's across from the post office.

   _____

3. Go to Grand Street. Turn left. It's next to the parking lot.

   _____

4. Go one block. Turn right on Grand Street. It's across from Ed's Restaurant.

   _____

🔘 **Listen and repeat.**

C Talk with a partner. Look at the map in Exercise B. Change the **bold** words and make conversations.

> **A** Excuse me. How do I get to the **DMV**?
> **B** **Go two blocks. Turn left.**
> **It's on Main Street.**
> **A** OK. **Go two blocks. Turn left.**
> **It's on Main Street.**
> **B** Right.
> **A** Thank you.

Culture note
The DMV is the Department of Motor Vehicles.
You can get a driver's license there.

1. DMV   3. drugstore   5. hospital
2. parking lot 4. library   6. post office

3 Communicate

Talk with a partner. Give directions to a building on the map in Exercise B.
Your partner names the building.

Go two blocks. Turn left. It's on Main Street.   The DMV.

Reading

1 Before you read

Talk. Look at these photos of Sandra's new neighborhood. Answer the questions.

1. What are the places in her neighborhood?
2. What can you do in these places?

2 Read

SELF-STUDY
AUDIO CD

Listen and read.

Hi Angela,

I love my new house. My neighborhood is great!
Here are some pictures.

There is a school on my street. My children go to the school.
They like it a lot. There is a community center across from the school.
My husband works at the community center. He walks to work. There is
a grocery store next to my house. It's a small store, but we can buy a lot
of things. There is a good Mexican restaurant on Second Street. It's right
across from my house.

I like it here, but I miss you. Please write.

Your friend,

Sandra

> When you see pronouns (*he, it, they*),
> ask *Who is the writer talking about?*
> Look at the sentences before a
> pronoun to find the answer.

3 After you read

A Read the sentences. Are they correct? Circle *Yes* or *No*.

1. Sandra lives on Summit Street.	Yes	(No)
2. There is a school on Sandra's street.	Yes	No
3. There is a community center next to the school.	Yes	No
4. Sandra's husband works at the community center.	Yes	No
5. Sandra's husband drives to work.	Yes	No

Write. Correct the sentences.

1. Sandra lives on <u>Second</u> Street.

B Write. Answer the questions about Sandra's neighborhood.

1. Where is the school? _____

2. Where is the grocery store? _____

3. Is the restaurant good? _____

Picture dictionary — Places around town

1. _a shopping mall_

2. _____

3. _____

4. _____

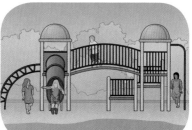

5. _____

6. _____

7. _____

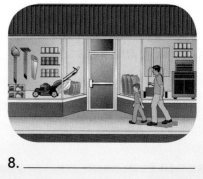

8. _____

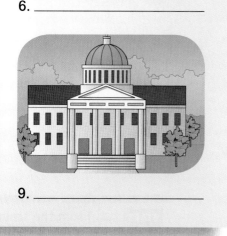

9. _____

SELF-STUDY AUDIO CD

A **Write** the words in the picture dictionary. Then listen and repeat.

an apartment building	a gas station	a playground
a courthouse	a hardware store	a police station
a day-care center	a high school	a shopping mall

B **Talk** with a partner about your neighborhood.

There's a gas station in my neighborhood.

Where is it?

It's across from the bank.

Culture note

Most elementary school students are 5 to 10 years old.

Most middle school students are 11 to 13 years old.

Most high school students are 14 to 18 years old.

Lesson E Writing

1 Before you write

A 🔘 **Listen.** Draw the way from the train station to the school.

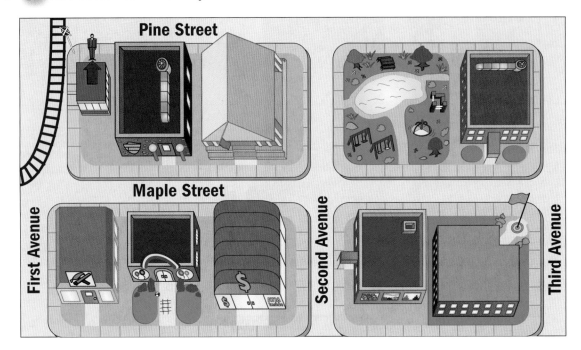

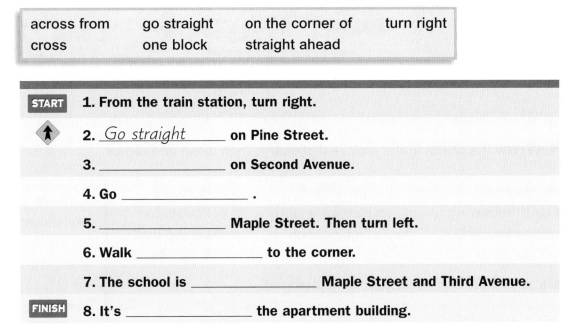

Write. Look at the map. Complete the directions from the train station to the school.

across from	go straight	on the corner of	turn right
cross	one block	straight ahead	

START 1. From the train station, turn right.

⬆ 2. _Go straight_____ on Pine Street.

3. _____ on Second Avenue.

4. Go _____ .

5. _____ Maple Street. Then turn left.

6. Walk _____ to the corner.

7. The school is _____ Maple Street and Third Avenue.

FINISH 8. It's _____ the apartment building.

Talk with a partner. Give different directions to get from the train station to the school.

66   Unit 5

B Write. Add capital letters.

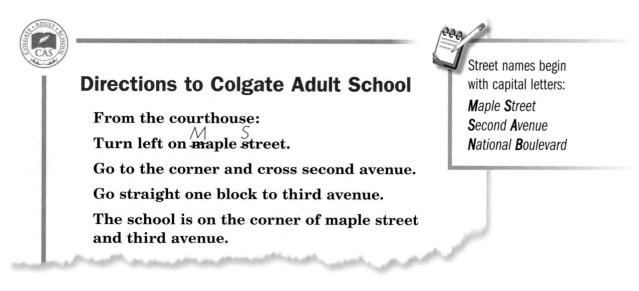

Directions to Colgate Adult School

From the courthouse:

Turn left on maple street. *(M, S)*

Go to the corner and cross second avenue.

Go straight one block to third avenue.

The school is on the corner of maple street and third avenue.

> Street names begin with capital letters:
> *Maple Street*
> *Second Avenue*
> *National Boulevard*

C Write. Work with a partner. Complete the chart. Write four streets near your school. Write four places near your school.

Streets	Places

2 Write

Draw a map first. Show directions to your school. Start from a bus stop, a train station, a subway stop, a restaurant, or your home.

Write the directions to your school.

3 After you write

A Read your directions to a partner.

B Check your partner's directions.
- What are the street names?
- Do all the street names have capital letters?

Another view

1 Life-skills reading

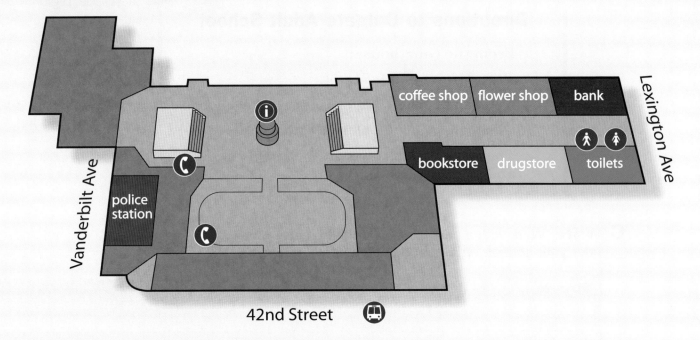

A **Read** the questions. Look at the map. Circle the answers.

1. Where is the drugstore?
   a. It's between the coffee shop and the bank.
   b. It's on Lexington Avenue.
   c. It's next to the bookstore.
   d. It's across from the coffee shop.

2. Where is the bus stop?
   a. It's on Lexington Avenue.
   b. It's on 42nd Street.
   c. It's on Vanderbilt Avenue.
   d. It's on the corner of Lexington Avenue and 42nd Street.

3. Where is the police station?
   a. It's on Vanderbilt Avenue.
   b. It's on 42nd Street.
   c. It's on Lexington Avenue.
   d. It's on the corner of Lexington Avenue and 42nd Street.

4. Where is the flower shop?
   a. It's next to the police station.
   b. It's across from the bookstore.
   c. It's between the coffee shop and the bank.
   d. It's on Vanderbilt Avenue.

B **Talk** with your classmates. Ask and answer the questions.

1. What places in your neighborhood do you go to every day?
2. Where do you go on the weekend?

2 Fun with language

A Work with a partner. Where do you find these things? Write the words.

| gas station | grocery store | library | restaurant |

1. _gas station_   2. _____   3. _____   4. _____

Write. What do you do in each place? Write sentences in your notebook.

1. I buy gas at the gas station.

B Work in a group. Solve the map puzzle. Read the clues. Write the names of the places.

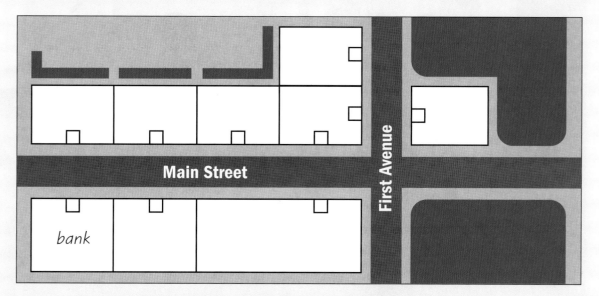

1. The day-care center is between the hospital and the bank.
2. The DMV is across from the hospital, on the corner of Main and First.
3. The courthouse is between the DMV and the library.
4. The post office is next to the library.
5. The gas station is next to the DMV.
6. The police station is across from the DMV.

3 Wrap up

Complete the **Self-assessment** on page 143.

Lesson A Get ready

1 Talk about the picture

A Look at the picture. What do you see?

B Point to a person: eating • talking • taking a nap • drinking coffee
reading a schedule • buying a snack

CHOKING
Emergency Care for

WIPE IT UP

NIGHT CHECKLIST

WORK SCHEDULE		
Margie Orlov	M, W, F T, Th	8-4 10-6
Bob Green	M-F	11-7
Andy Mapes	T-Sat	12-8
Ricardo Suarez	M, W, F T, Th	10-6 8-4

Bob

2 Listening

SELF-STUDY AUDIO CD

A 🔊 **Listen.** Circle the words you hear.

buy a snack	eat dinner	start work
catch the bus	get home	take a break
drink coffee	(leave for work)	take a nap

SELF-STUDY AUDIO CD

B 💿 **Listen again.** Write the letter of the conversation.

1. ____   2. ____   3. ____

4. ____   5. ____   6. _a_

Listen again. Check your answers.

C 🔊 **Listen** and repeat the times.

What time is it?   It's ten o'clock.

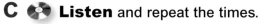

1. ten o'clock   2. ten-thirty   3. six-fifteen   4. five-twenty

5. twelve-fifty   6. two-forty-five   7. seven-thirty   8. nine-oh-five

Talk with a partner. Take turns. Ask and tell the time.

What do you do in the evening?

1 Grammar focus: simple present tense; *Wh-* questions

Questions			Answers		With *he* and *she*:
What	do you do does he do does she do do they do	in the evening?	I He She They	read. reads. reads. read.	do → does exercise → exercises go → goes study → studies watch → watches

2 Practice

A Write. Complete the sentences. Use *do* or *does* and the correct form of the verb.

A What _do_ they do in the evening?

B They _____*watch*_____ TV.
(watch / watches)

A What _____ he do in the afternoon?

B He _____ .
(study / studies)

A What _____ she do in the morning?

B She _____ .
(exercise / exercises)

A What _____ they do on Sunday?

B They _____ to the park.
(go / goes)

Listen and repeat. Then practice with a partner.

B 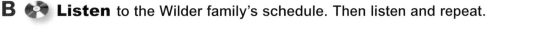 **Listen** to the Wilder family's schedule. Then listen and repeat.

SATURDAY MORNING	SATURDAY AFTERNOON	SATURDAY EVENING
Jill watches TV.	She plays soccer.	She listens to music.
Mr. and Mrs. Wilder go shopping.	They work in the garden.	They pay bills.

Listen. Then talk with a partner. Change the **bold words** and make conversations.

> **A** What does **Jill** do on **Saturday morning**?
> **B** **She** usually **watches TV**.

1. Jill / Saturday morning
2. Mr. and Mrs. Wilder / Saturday evening
3. Mr. and Mrs. Wilder / Saturday morning
4. Jill / Saturday afternoon
5. Mr. and Mrs. Wilder / Saturday afternoon
6. Jill / Saturday evening

3 Communicate

Talk with your classmates. Ask questions about the weekend.

What do you do on Saturday morning?

I usually go to the grocery store.

> **Useful language**
> *Usually* means *most of the time.*
> *Always* means *all of the time.*

I go to work at 8:00.

1 Grammar focus: *at*, *in*, and *on* with time; *When* questions

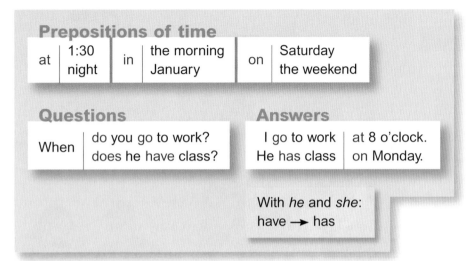

Prepositions of time

at	1:30 night	in	the morning January	on	Saturday the weekend

Questions

When	do you go to work? does he have class?

Answers

I go to work He has class	at 8 o'clock. on Monday.

With *he* and *she*:
have → has

2 Practice

A Write. Complete the sentences.
Use *at*, *in*, or *on*.

1. I have English class _on_ Tuesday and Thursday.

2. My sister has class ____ Saturday.

3. I do homework ____ night.

4. My father goes to work ____ the morning.

5. He catches the bus ____ 8:45.

6. Sometimes my mom goes to PTA meetings ____ the evening.

7. I go on vacation ____ July.

Culture note
The PTA is the Parent-Teacher Association at a school. Parents and teachers meet in a group to talk about school.

B Write. Read the answers. Complete the questions.

1. **A** When ___do___ you ___go___ on vacation?
   B I go on vacation in July.

2. **A** When _____ your sister _____ class?
   B She has class on Saturday.

3. **A** When _____ your father _____ the bus?
   B He catches the bus at 8:45.

4. **A** When _____ you _____ homework?
   B I do homework at night.

Listen and repeat. Then practice with a partner.

C 🔊 **Listen.** Then talk with a partner. Change the bold words and make conversations.

Mrs. Wilder's Schedule

SUNDAY	MONDAY	TUESDAY	WEDNESDAY	THURSDAY	FRIDAY	SATURDAY
rest	11:00 a.m. volunteer at the high school	7:30 p.m. cooking class	2:30 p.m. driving lessons	4:00 p.m. Spanish class	6:30 p.m. PTA meeting	9:00 a.m. go shopping

A When does Mrs. Wilder **volunteer at the high school**?
B She **volunteers at the high school on Monday**.
A What time?
B At **11:00 in the morning**.

Culture note

Many people in the U.S. do volunteer work in their free time. Volunteers do not receive money for their work.

1. volunteer at the high school
2. take driving lessons
3. have cooking class
4. have Spanish class
5. go shopping
6. go to the PTA meeting

Useful language

She **has** cooking class on Tuesday.
She **goes to** cooking class on Tuesday.

3 Communicate

Write. What are five things you do every week? Make a list.

1. call my mother
2. go to English class
3. work
4. visit friends
5. go to the grocery store

Talk with a partner. Ask questions about your partner's list.

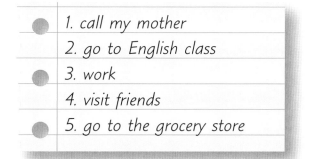

When do you call your mother?

I usually call my mother on Sunday at nine o'clock at night.

Lesson D Reading

1 Before you read

Talk. Bob has a new job. Look at the picture. Answer the questions.

1. What is Bob wearing?
2. What is his new job?

2 Read

SELF-STUDY AUDIO CD

Listen and read.

Meet Our New Employee: Bob Green

Please welcome Bob. He is a new security guard. He works the night shift at the East End Factory. Bob starts work at 11:00 at night. He leaves work at 7:00 in the morning.

Bob likes these hours because he can spend time with his family. Bob says, "I eat breakfast with my wife, Arlene, and my son, Brett, at 7:30 every morning. I help Brett with his homework in the afternoon. I eat dinner with my family at 6:30. Then we watch TV. At 10:30, I go to work."

Congratulations to Bob on his new job!

To help you remember, ask questions as you read:

Who is this reading about?
What is this reading about?
Where does Bob work?
When does Bob work?

3 After you read

A Read the sentences. Are they correct? Circle *Yes* or *No*.

1. Bob is a new police officer.	Yes	(No)
2. He starts work at 7:00 at night.	Yes	No
3. He likes to spend time with his family.	Yes	No
4. Bob helps Brett with his homework.	Yes	No
5. Bob's family eats dinner at 6:30.	Yes	No
6. At 10:30, Bob watches TV.	Yes	No

Write. Correct the sentences.

1. Bob is a new <u>security guard</u>.

B Write. Answer the questions about Bob's schedule.

1. When does Bob eat breakfast with his family? _____

2. Where does Bob work? _____

Picture dictionary   Daily activities

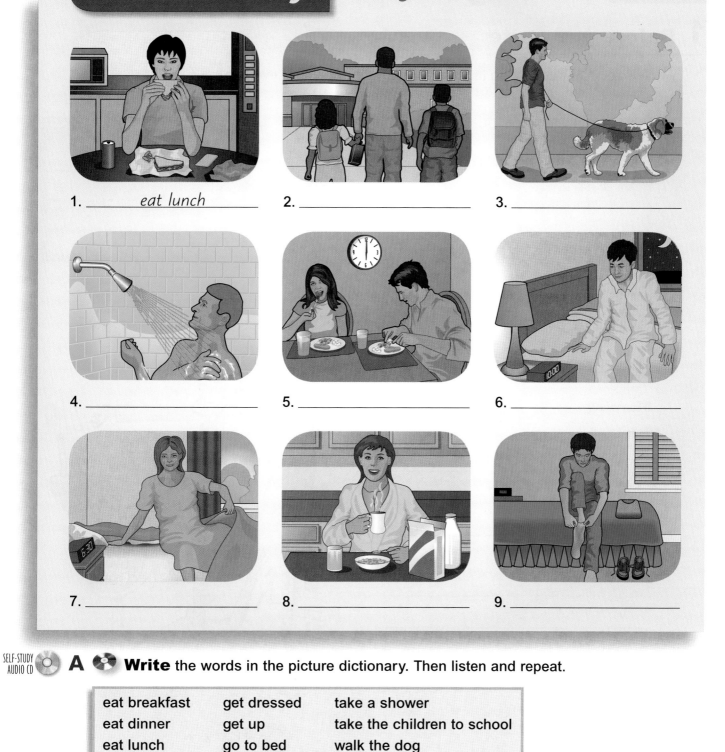

1. _____eat lunch_____   2. _____   3. _____

4. _____   5. _____   6. _____

7. _____   8. _____   9. _____

SELF-STUDY
AUDIO CD

A **Write** the words in the picture dictionary. Then listen and repeat.

eat breakfast	get dressed	take a shower
eat dinner	get up	take the children to school
eat lunch	go to bed	walk the dog

B **Talk** with a partner. Ask and answer questions about your daily activities.

When do you eat breakfast?   I usually eat breakfast at 6:30.

1 Before you write

A Write. What do you do in the morning, afternoon, and evening?
Complete the chart.

Morning	Afternoon	Evening
get up		
get dressed		

Talk with a partner about your daily schedule.

What do you do in the morning?   I get up. I get dressed. . . .

Write sentences.

Morning

I get up.

I get dressed.

_____

_____

Afternoon

_____

_____

_____

_____

Evening

_____

_____

_____

_____

B Write. Complete the paragraph. Use *in*, *on*, and *at*.

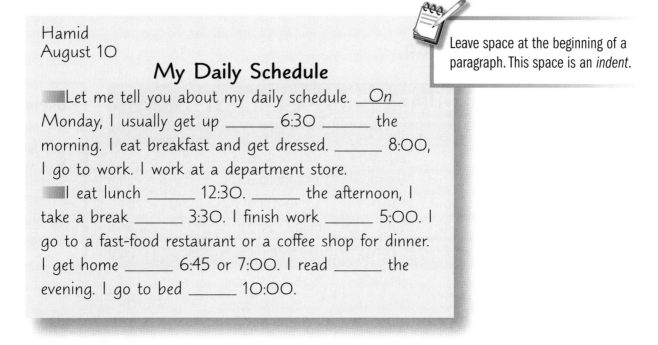

Hamid
August 10

My Daily Schedule

    Let me tell you about my daily schedule. <u>On</u> Monday, I usually get up _____ 6:30 _____ the morning. I eat breakfast and get dressed. _____ 8:00, I go to work. I work at a department store.

    I eat lunch _____ 12:30. _____ the afternoon, I take a break _____ 3:30. I finish work _____ 5:00. I go to a fast-food restaurant or a coffee shop for dinner. I get home _____ 6:45 or 7:00. I read _____ the evening. I go to bed _____ 10:00.

Leave space at the beginning of a paragraph. This space is an *indent*.

2 Write

Write a paragraph about your daily schedule.

3 After you write

A Read your paragraph to a partner.

B Check your partner's paragraph.

• What does your partner do in the evening?
• Is there an indent at the beginning of the paragraph?

1 Life-skills reading

CLASS SCHEDULE: SPRING SEMESTER

BUSINESS			
Business English	MTuWThF	5:00–7:30 p.m.	3/17–5/22
Keyboarding	MWF	1:00–3:00 p.m.	1/14–5/25
Introduction to Computers	TuTh	10:30–12:30 p.m.	3/17–5/24
Word Processing	TuTh	6:30–9:30 p.m.	3/17–5/24

ENGLISH AS A SECOND LANGUAGE			
ESL Beginning	MTuWThF	8:15–10:15 a.m.	1/15–5/25
ESL Intermediate	MTuWThF	8:15–10:15 p.m.	1/15–5/25
ESL Citizenship	Sat	8:00–10:45 a.m.	1/20–5/19
ESL Citizenship	Sun	7:45–10:30 a.m.	1/21–5/20
ESL Pronunciation	MWF	12:00–1:00 p.m.	3/19–5/25
ESL Writing	MTuWTh	12:00–1:15 p.m.	3/19–5/24

Useful language

M	Monday
Tu	Tuesday
W	Wednesday
Th	Thursday
F	Friday
Sat	Saturday
Sun	Sunday

A Read the questions. Look at the schedule. Circle the answers.

1. What time does the ESL Citizenship class start on Saturday morning?
   a. at 7:45
   b. at 8:00
   c. at 8:15
   d. at 10:15

2. When does the Introduction to Computers class start?
   a. on January 15
   b. on February 12
   c. on March 17
   d. on March 19

3. When is the ESL Pronunciation class?
   a. on Monday, Wednesday, and Friday
   b. on Tuesday and Thursday
   c. on Monday, Tuesday, and Thursday
   d. on Monday, Tuesday, and Wednesday

4. When does the spring semester end?
   a. in January
   b. in February
   c. in March
   d. in May

B Talk with a partner. Ask and answer questions about the schedule.

What time does the Business English class start? | It starts at five o'clock.

2 Fun with language

A Work in a group. Look at a calendar for this year. Find the holidays. Write the day of the week for each holiday.

Holiday	When	Day of the week
New Year's Day	January 1	1. _____
Valentine's Day	February 14	2. _____
Independence Day	July 4	3. _____
Veterans Day	November 11	4. _____

B Work in a group. Look at a calendar for this year. Find the holidays. Write the date for each holiday.

Holiday	When	Date this year
Mother's Day	2nd Sunday in May	1. _____
Father's Day	3rd Sunday in June	2. _____
Thanksgiving Day	4th Thursday in November	3. _____
Labor Day	1st Monday in September	4. _____

C Write. Do you celebrate other holidays? Write three other holidays.

Holiday	When	Date this year

Talk with your classmates. Ask and answers questions about the holidays.

1. What is the name of the holiday?
2. When is it?
3. What do you eat on this holiday?
4. What do you do on this holiday? How do you celebrate?

3 Wrap up

Complete the **Self-assessment** on page 143.

Review

1 Listening

Read the questions. Then listen and circle the answers.

1. Where is the DMV?
   a. on Broadway
   b. on Fifth Avenue

2. What is the address number?
   a. 550
   b. 515

3. Is the DMV between the coffee shop and the grocery store?
   a. Yes, it is.
   b. No, it isn't.

4. Is the DMV between the bank and the coffee shop?
   a. Yes, it is.
   b. No, it isn't.

5. Is the DMV across from the hospital?
   a. Yes, it is.
   b. No, it isn't.

Talk with a partner. Ask and answer the questions. Use complete sentences.

2 Grammar

A Write. Complete the story.

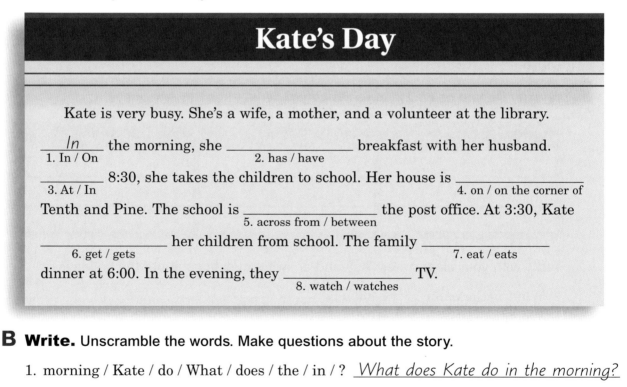

Kate's Day

Kate is very busy. She's a wife, a mother, and a volunteer at the library.

___In___ the morning, she _____ breakfast with her husband.
1. In / On   2. has / have

_____ 8:30, she takes the children to school. Her house is _____
3. At / In   4. on / on the corner of

Tenth and Pine. The school is _____ the post office. At 3:30, Kate
5. across from / between

_____ her children from school. The family _____
6. get / gets   7. eat / eats

dinner at 6:00. In the evening, they _____ TV.
8. watch / watches

B Write. Unscramble the words. Make questions about the story.

1. morning / Kate / do / What / does / the / in / ? _What does Kate do in the morning?_

2. school / Where / the / is / ? _____

3. get / When / children / does / her / Kate / ? _____

4. What time / the family / eat / dinner / does / ? _____

_____

Talk with a partner. Ask and answer the questions.

3 Pronunciation: intonation in questions

A 🔊 **Listen** to the intonation in these questions.

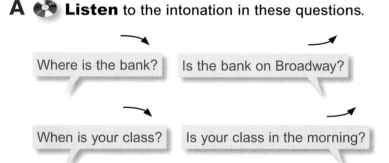

Where is the bank? Is the bank on Broadway?

When is your class? Is your class in the morning?

B 🔊 **Listen and repeat.**

Wh- questions

1. **A** Where is the post office?
   B It's on First Street.

2. **A** What time do they eat dinner?
   B They eat dinner at 6:30.

Yes / No questions

3. **A** Are you from Mexico?
   B Yes, I am.

4. **A** Does he start work at 7:00?
   B No, he doesn't.

C **Talk** with a partner. Ask and answer the questions.

1. What time do you go to bed?
2. When is your birthday?
3. Where is your supermarket?
4. What time is your English class?
5. Do you visit your friends on the weekend?
6. Do you work in the evening?
7. Do you volunteer?
8. Do you watch TV in the afternoon?

D **Write** five questions.

   What's your name?

1. _____

2. _____

3. _____

4. _____

5. _____

Talk with a partner. Ask and answer the questions. Use correct intonation.

What's your name? My name is Teresa.

1 Talk about the picture

A Look at the picture. What do you see?

B Point to: apples • bananas • bread • cheese • cookies • milk
a cashier • a shopping cart • a stock clerk

Shopping

Shirley

Dan

2 Listening

SELF-STUDY AUDIO CD

A **Listen.** Circle the words you hear.

apples	bread	cookies	onions	rice
bananas	cheese	(milk)	potatoes	rice tomatoes

SELF-STUDY AUDIO CD

B **Listen again.** Write the letter of the conversation.

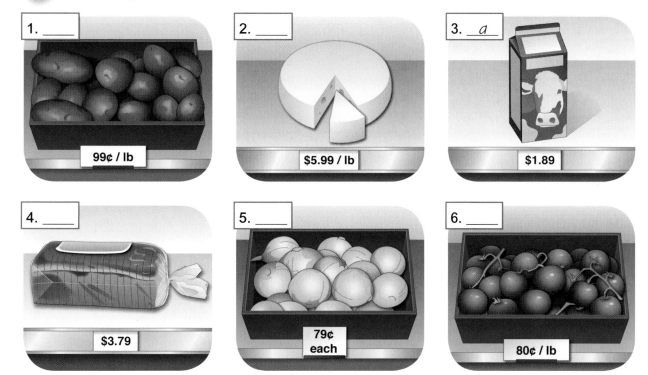

1. ____ 99¢ / lb

2. ____ $5.99 / lb

3. _a_ $1.89

4. ____ $3.79

5. ____ 79¢ each

6. ____ 80¢ / lb

Listen again. Check your answers.

C **Write.** Add the prices of all the items. What is the total?

```
potatoes - 2lb      $1.98
onions  - 1           .79
tomatoes - 3lb       2.40
cheese  - 1lb        5.99
bread   - 1          3.79
milk    - 2          3.78


Total       $ _____ . ___


Thank you!
```

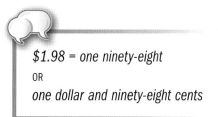

$1.98 = one ninety-eight
OR
one dollar and ninety-eight cents

How many? How much?

1 Grammar focus: count / non-count nouns; *How many? / How much?*

Questions		Answers		
How many apples	do we need?	We need	one apple. two apples.	We don't need any.
How much milk	do we need?	We need	a lot of milk.	We don't need any.

Count nouns

an apple	a cookie	an orange
a banana	an egg	a peach
a carrot	an onion	a pie

Non-count nouns

bread	juice	rice
cheese	meat	sugar
coffee	milk	water

2 Practice

A Look at the pictures. Circle only the count nouns.

1   2   3   4

5   6   7   8

9   10   11   12

Listen and repeat.

B Write. Look at the pictures on page 86. Write the food words on the chart.

1. *carrots*	5.	9.
2. *water*	6.	10.
3.	7.	11.
4.	8.	12.

C Write. Complete the questions. Use *many* or *much*.

1. How __*many*__ eggs do we need?
2. How __*much*__ juice do we need?
3. How _____ milk do we need?
4. How _____ pies do we need?
5. How _____ bread do we need?
6. How _____ potatoes do we need?
7. How _____ rice do we need?
8. How _____ meat do we need?

 **Listen and repeat.**

D Talk with a partner. Change the bold words and make conversations.

> **A** We need **apples**.
> **B** How **many apples** do we need?
> **A** Two.

1. apples / two
2. milk / not much
3. bananas / five
4. bread / a lot
5. oranges / six
6. cheese / not much
7. eggs / a dozen
8. onions / not many

> **A** We need **milk**.
> **B** How **much milk** do we need?
> **A** **Not much.**

Useful language

How many *do we need?*
You can answer *Not many* OR *A lot.*

How much *do we need?*
You can answer *Not much* OR *A lot.*

3 Communicate

Talk with a partner. Pretend you are making a fruit salad for four friends.
Check (✓) six items. Then make conversations.

> How many apples do we need?   We need three.

- ☐ apples
- ☐ bananas
- ☐ blueberries
- ☐ cherries
- ☐ orange juice
- ☐ oranges
- ☐ pineapples
- ☐ strawberries
- ☐ sugar

Lesson C · Are there any bananas?

1 Grammar focus: *There is / There are*

Statements

There is	a banana	on the table.
There are	two bananas	
There is	bread	on the table.

Questions

Is there	a banana	on the table?
Are there	any bananas	
Is there	any bread	on the table?

Answers

Yes, there	is.	No, there	isn't.
	are.		aren't.
Yes, there	is.	No, there	isn't.

2 Practice

A Write. Complete the sentences. Use *there is*, *there are*, *there isn't*, or *there aren't*.

1. **A** Is there any bread on the table?
   B Yes, _____ _____ .

2. **A** Are there any eggs?
   B No, _____ _____ .

3. **A** Is there any juice?
   B Yes, _____ _____ .

4. **A** Is there any water?
   B No, _____ _____ .

5. **A** Are there any cookies?
   B Yes, _____ _____ .

6. **A** Are there any bananas?
   B No, _____ _____ .

Listen and repeat. Then practice with a partner.

B Write. Complete the questions. Use *Is there* or *Are there*.

1. **A** _____ _____ any meat in the refrigerator?
   B Yes, there is.

2. **A** _____ _____ any oranges?
   B Yes, there are.

3. **A** _____ _____ any cheese?
   B No, there isn't.

4. **A** _____ _____ any coffee?
   B Yes, there is.

5. **A** _____ _____ any apples?
   B No, there aren't.

6. **A** _____ _____ any cherries?
   B Yes, there are.

Listen and repeat. Then practice with a partner.

C Write. Complete the sentences. Use *There is* or *There are*.

Useful language

You can count words like *loaf*, *carton*, *box*, *bottle*, *package*, *can*, and *bag*.

Use these words with non-count nouns.

1. ___There___ ___is___ one loaf of bread.
2. _____ _____ two cartons of apple juice.
3. _____ _____ three boxes of tea.
4. _____ _____ four bottles of water.

5. _____ _____ one package of ground meat.
6. _____ _____ six cans of soda.
7. _____ _____ one bag of flour.
8. _____ _____ two packages of cheese.

Listen and repeat.

D Talk with a partner. Look at the picture. Make conversations.

Is there any rice?

Yes, there is a bag of rice on the shelf.

Is there any soda?

No, there isn't.

1. rice	3. milk	5. tea	7. sugar
2. soda	4. coffee	6. cheese	8. water

3 Communicate

Talk with a partner. Ask and answer these questions.

1. What is in your refrigerator?
2. What is on your kitchen shelves?

Reading

1 Before you read

Talk. Shirley and Dan are shopping. Look at the picture. Answer the questions.

1. Where are they?
2. What are they doing?

2 Read

SELF-STUDY
AUDIO CD **Listen and read.**

Regular Customers

Shirley and Dan are regular customers at SaveMore Supermarket. They go to SaveMore three or four times a week. The cashiers and stock clerks at SaveMore know them and like them. There are fruit and vegetables, meat and fish, and cookies and cakes in the supermarket. But today, Shirley and Dan are buying apples, bananas, bread, and cheese. There is one problem. The total is $16.75. They only have a ten-dollar bill, 5 one-dollar bills, and three quarters!

When you don't understand a word, look for clues.
Do you understand *regular customer*?
Clue: They go to SaveMore *three or four times a week.*

3 After you read

A Read the sentences. Are they correct? Circle *Yes* or *No*.

1. Shirley and Dan go to SaveMore three or four times a day.	Yes	(No)
2. They are regular customers at SaveMore Supermarket.	Yes	No
3. The cashiers and stock clerks know them.	Yes	No
4. Shirley and Dan are buying meat and fish.	Yes	No
5. Shirley and Dan have $16.00.	Yes	No

B Write. Correct the sentences.

1. Shirley and Dan go to SaveMore three or four times a <u>week</u>.

C Write. Answer the questions about Shirley and Dan.

1. How much money do Shirley and Dan have? _____

2. How many quarters do they have? _____

3. How much more money do they need? _____

4

Picture dictionary · Money

1. _a penny_

2. _____

3. _____

4. _____

5. _____

6. _____

7. _____

8. _____

9. _____

10. _____

11. _____

12. _____

SELF-STUDY AUDIO CD

A **Write** the words in the picture dictionary. Then listen and repeat.

an ATM card	a dime	a nickel	a quarter
a check	a five-dollar bill	a one-dollar bill	a ten-dollar bill
a credit card	a half-dollar	a penny	a twenty-dollar bill

B **Talk** with a partner. Look at the pictures.
Change the **bold** words and make conversations.

> **A** Do you have change for **a dollar**?
> **B** Sure. What do you need?
> **A** I need **four quarters**.
> **B** Here you are.

You can say:
a one-dollar bill OR _a dollar_
a five-dollar bill OR _five dollars_
a ten-dollar bill OR _ten dollars_

1

2

3

4

Shopping   **91**

Lesson E *Writing*

1 Before you write

A Talk with a partner. Ask and answer questions.

1. When do you go shopping?
2. What are the names of some supermarkets in your neighborhood?
3. What do you usually buy at the supermarket?

B Read the note. Make a shopping list.

> Hi Mom,
>
> Please stop at SaveMore on your way home. I'm making spaghetti for dinner.
>
> There is cheese in the refrigerator. There are two peppers next to the stove. But there aren't any onions. I need two. And I need four carrots, six tomatoes, a carton of milk, and a package of ground meat.
>
> Thanks.
>
> Kate

Going shopping:

2 onions

_____

_____

_____

_____

C Write. Look at the picture. What is she buying? Write the words.

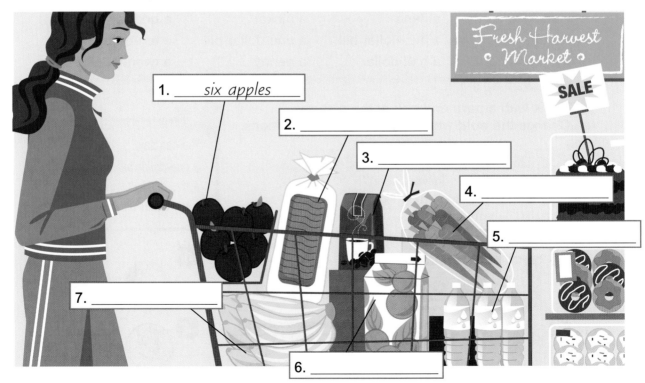

1. ___six apples___
2. _____
3. _____
4. _____
5. _____
6. _____
7. _____

D Write. Correct the note. Add commas.

Hi Roberto,

I'm making dinner tonight, but I need a few more groceries. I need a package of meat an onion a green pepper three tomatoes and a bag of rice. I also need a carton of milk two bottles of apple juice six cans of soda and a carton of orange juice. Oh, and one more thing — a dozen eggs.

Thanks. See you tonight.

Iris

Put a comma (,) after each item when there is a list of three or more items.

Please buy five oranges, two apples, and a peach.

2 Write

Write a note asking someone to go shopping for you.

3 After you write

A Read your note to a partner.

B Check your partner's note.
- What food does your partner need?
- Are the commas correct?

Another view

1 Life-skills reading

A **Read** the questions. Look at the ad. Circle the answers.

1. What's the name of the store?
   a. SaveMore Supermarket
   b. The Place to Shop
   c. This week only
   d. Fourth of July Blowout

2. How much are paper plates?
   a. 10¢
   b. $1.39
   c. $3.95
   d. $4.49

3. How much are Florida oranges?
   a. 50¢
   b. $1.00
   c. $2.00
   d. $4.00

4. How much are Yummy Soft Drinks?
   a. 79¢
   b. $1.19
   c. $1.58
   d. $2.37

B **Talk** in a group. Ask about the prices of different items in the ad.

> How much are the bananas?   They're sixty-nine cents a pound.

2 Fun with language

A **Work in a group.** Read the ad on page 94. Plan a party.
You have $30.00. What do you want to buy? Make a list. Add the total.

Read your list to the class. What is the total?

B **Work in a group.** What food is in each category? Write some names.

Fats, Oils, and Sweets

1. _____ 2. _____ 3. _____

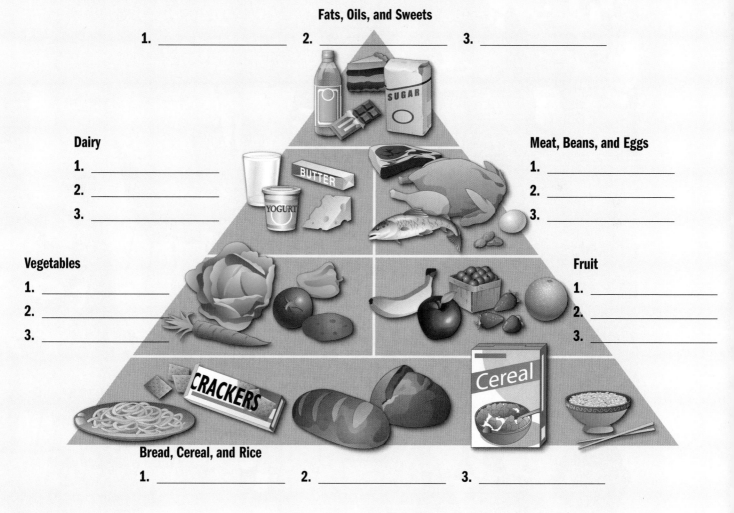

Dairy

1. _____
2. _____
3. _____

Meat, Beans, and Eggs

1. _____
2. _____
3. _____

Vegetables

1. _____
2. _____
3. _____

Fruit

1. _____
2. _____
3. _____

Bread, Cereal, and Rice

1. _____ 2. _____ 3. _____

3 Wrap up

Complete the **Self-assessment** on page 144.

Lesson **A** *Get ready*

1 Talk about the picture

A Look at the picture. What do you see?

B Point to: a busboy • a waiter • a construction worker • a cook
a nurse • a nursing assistant • a cashier

Work

Mai Linh

2 Listening

SELF-STUDY AUDIO CD **A** 🔘 **Listen.** Circle the words you hear.

busboy	electrician	receptionist
cashier	nurse	truck driver
doctor	office worker	(waitress)

SELF-STUDY AUDIO CD **B** 🔘 **Listen again.** Write the letter of the conversation.

1. _____ 2. _a_

3. _____ 4. _____

5. _____ 6. _____

Listen again. Check your answers.

C Write. Where do the people work? Write the words.

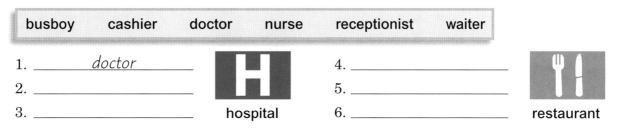

busboy	cashier	doctor	nurse	receptionist	waiter

1. _____doctor_____ 4. _____
2. _____ 5. _____
3. _____ 6. _____

hospital restaurant

I was a teacher.

1 Grammar focus: simple past of *be*

Questions			Answers			
Were	you	a student?		I was.		I wasn't. I was a teacher.
Was	he	a student?		he was.		he wasn't. He was a teacher.
Was	she	a student?	Yes,	she was.	No,	she wasn't. She was a teacher.
Were	they	students?		they were.		they weren't. They were teachers.

wasn't = was not   weren't = were not

2 Practice

A Write. Look at the pictures. Complete the sentences. Use *is*, *are*, *was*, or *were*.

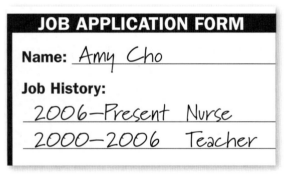

1. She ___was___ a teacher before.
   Now she ___is___ a nurse.

2. She _____ a manager now.
   She _____ a cashier before.

APPLICATION FORM

Name: BEN LIAO

Job History:

2006 – PRESENT CONSTRUCTION WORKER

2004 – 2006 WAITER

3. They _____ students before.
   Now they _____ electricians.

4. He _____ a waiter before.
   Now he _____ a construction worker.

 **Listen and repeat.**

B Talk with a partner. Look at the pictures. Change the **bold** words and make conversations.

1. **A** Was **she a teacher**?
   B Yes, **she** was.

2. **A** Were they **receptionists**?
   B No, they weren't. They were **nurses**.

1. a teacher?

2. receptionists?

3. waiter?

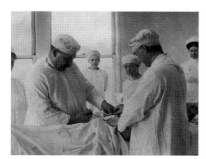

4. electricians?

5. a cook?

6. a cashier?

3 Communicate

Talk with three classmates. Complete the chart.

> **A** Sylvia, what do you do now?
> **B** Now? I'm a housewife.
> **A** Oh, really? Were you a housewife before?
> **B** No, I wasn't. I was a receptionist in a bank.

Useful language

In conversation, *What do you do?* means *What's your job?* OR *What's your occupation?*

Name	Job now	Job before
Sylvia	a housewife	a receptionist

Write two sentences about your classmates. Use information from the chart.

Sylvia is a housewife now. She was a receptionist before.

Lesson C Can you cook?

1 Grammar focus: *can*

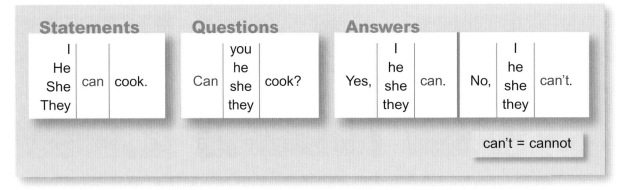

Statements			Questions			Answers					
I He She They	can	cook.	Can	you he she they	cook?	Yes,	I he she they	can.	No,	I he she they	can't.

can't = cannot

2 Practice

A Write. Complete the sentences. Use *yes*, *no*, *can*, or *can't*.

A Can she speak Spanish?
B ___Yes___ , she ___can___ .

A Can he drive a truck?
B ___No___ , he ___can't___ .

A Can he fix a car?
B _____ , he _____ .

A Can she paint a house?
B _____ , she _____ .

A Can they work with computers?
B _____ , they _____ .

A Can you cook?
B _____ , I _____ .

🔘 **Listen and repeat.** Then practice with a partner.

100   Unit 8

B Write. Look at the pictures. Complete the sentences.

build things	paint	take care of children
fix cars	sell	take care of plants

1. A painter can
   paint .

2. A salesperson can
   _____ .

3. A carpenter can
   _____ .

4. A gardener can
   _____ .

5. A child-care worker can
   _____ .

6. An auto mechanic can
   _____ .

🔊 **Listen and repeat.**

C Talk with a partner. Look at the pictures in Exercise B. Change the **bold** words and make conversations.

> **A** Hi. I'm looking for a job. Can you help me?
> **B** What can you do?
> **A** I'm **a painter**. I can **paint** very well.

3 Communicate

Talk with a partner. Ask and answer questions.

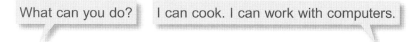

What can you do? | I can cook. I can work with computers.

Lesson D Reading

1 Before you read

Talk. Mai Linh is looking for a new job. Look at the picture. Answer the questions.

1. Who are the people in the picture?
2. Where are they?
3. What is Mai Linh's volunteer job now?

Harmon Hills Nursing Home

Valley Adult School

2 Read

SELF-STUDY AUDIO CD **Listen and read.**

Dear Ms. Carter:

   I am writing this letter to recommend my student Mai Linh Lam.

   Mai Linh was a teacher in Vietnam. She is looking for a new job in the United States. She is a certified nursing assistant now. She volunteers in a nursing home Monday through Friday from 8:30 to 4:30. She takes care of senior citizens.

   Mai has many good work skills. She can write reports. She can help elderly people move around and sit down. She can help them eat. She can also speak English and Vietnamese. These skills are useful in her job, and she is very good at her work.

Sincerely,
Elaine Maxwell

Verb forms can tell you if something happened in the past or is happening now.
*Mai Linh **was** a teacher in Vietnam.*
*She **is looking** for a new job.*

3 After you read

A Read the sentences. Are they correct? Circle *Yes* or *No*.

1. Mai Linh is looking for a job in Vietnam.   Yes   (No)
2. She volunteers in a hospital.   Yes   No
3. She can write reports.   Yes   No
4. She finishes work at 8:30.   Yes   No
5. She is good at her job.   Yes   No

Write. Correct the sentences.

1. Mai Linh is looking for a job in the United States.

B Write. Answer the questions about Mai Linh.

1. What was Mai Linh's job before? _____
2. Is Mai Linh certified? _____
3. What are her work skills? _____

Culture note
For some jobs, you need a certificate. You have to take a test to get the certificate. *I'm certified* means *I have a certificate.*

Picture dictionary — Occupations

1. _housekeeper_

2. _____

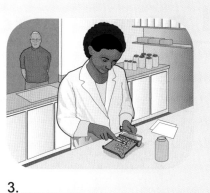
3. _____

4. _____

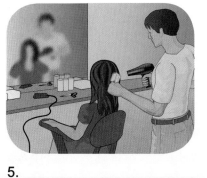
5. _____

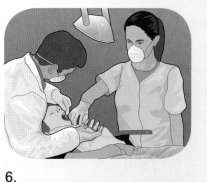
6. _____

A  **Write** the words in the picture dictionary. Then listen and repeat.

custodian	factory worker	housekeeper
dental assistant	hairstylist	pharmacist

B Work with a partner. Match the words in the picture dictionary with the places in the box.

1. a beauty salon
   hairstylist

2. a dental office
   _____

3. a factory
   _____

4. a hotel
   _____

5. an office building
   _____

6. a drugstore
   _____

Talk with a partner. Point to a picture in the dictionary. Ask and answer questions about the occupations.

What's her occupation?   She's a housekeeper.

Where does she work?   She works in a hotel.

Writing

1 Before you write

A **Write.** Check (✓) the boxes.

	Work skill	Life skill	Both
1. drive	☐	☐	☑
2. cook	☐	☐	☐
3. use a computer	☐	☐	☐
4. housework	☐	☐	☐
5. read to children	☐	☐	☐
6. pay bills	☐	☐	☐
7. shop	☐	☐	☐
8. read a schedule	☐	☐	☐

Talk with a partner.

A What about number 1? Can you drive?
B Yes, I can.
A Is it a work skill or a life skill?
B I think it's both.

B **Read.** Answer the questions.

Subject: My Skills

Date: Tues. 25 August 2007
From: CARLA <colsen@cup.org>
Subject: My Skills
To: ventures@cambridge.org

   My name is Carla. I am a housewife. I work at home. I have good life skills and work skills. I can do housework. I can drive a car, and I can fix a car, too. I can speak two languages. I can cook tasty meals for my family. I can help my children with their homework, and I can use a computer.

1. What are Carla's life skills? _____

   _____

2. What are Carla's work skills? _____

   _____

2 Write

A **Write** about your job. Complete the sentences.

I am a _____ .

I work at _____ .

B **Write.** What are your life skills and work skills? Make a list.

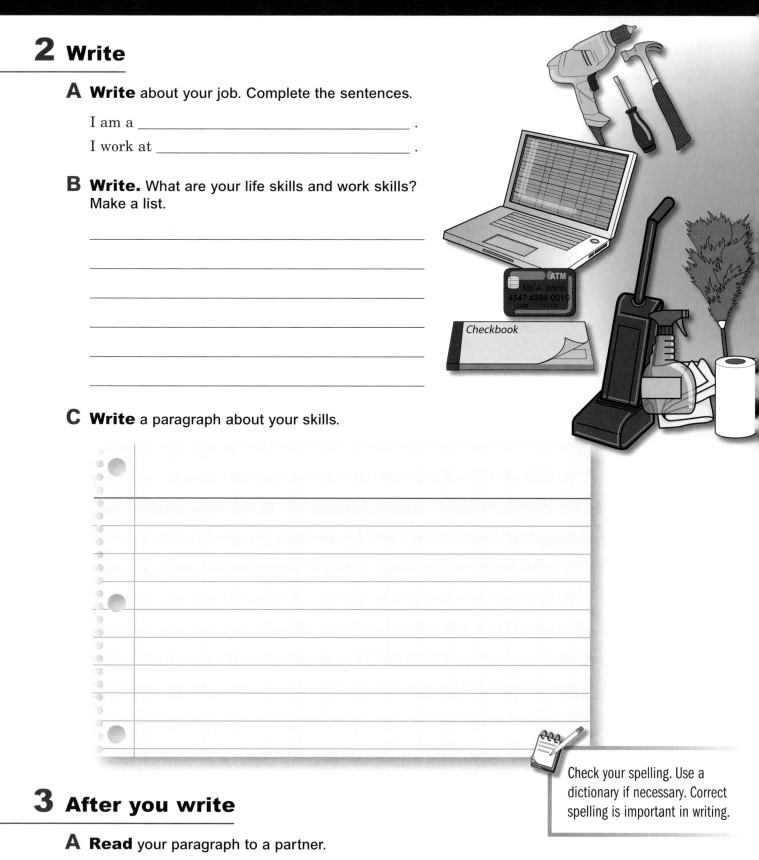

_____

_____

_____

_____

_____

_____

C **Write** a paragraph about your skills.

Check your spelling. Use a dictionary if necessary. Correct spelling is important in writing.

3 After you write

A **Read** your paragraph to a partner.

B **Check** your partner's paragraph.

- What are your partner's life skills?
- What are your partner's work skills?
- Is the spelling correct?

1 Life-skills reading

APPLICATION FOR EMPLOYMENT

1 Name _____
FIRST   LAST

2 Soc. Sec. No. _000-99-9103_

3 Address _____
STREET

4 Phone (_____) _____

_____
CITY   STATE   ZIP

5 Are you 16 years or older? Yes __ No __

6 Position desired _____

EMPLOYMENT HISTORY (List most recent job first.)

Dates	Employer Name and Address	Position

7 _____

8 _____

9 _____

10 **Important:** Show your Social Security card at the time you present this application.

A Read the questions. Look at the job application. Circle the answers.

1. Where do you write the job you want?
   a. line 5
   b. line 6
   c. line 8
   d. line 10

2. Where do you write your job now?
   a. line 5
   b. line 7
   c. line 8
   d. line 9

3. What do you show with your application?
   a. a library card
   b. a photograph
   c. a driver's license
   d. a Social Security card

4. Where do you write your phone number?
   a. line 4
   b. line 5
   c. line 8
   d. line 9

B Write. Complete the form with your own information.

C Talk with a partner about your form.

> My name is Mario Rivera. My address is 613 Apple Road, Los Angeles, California. I'm looking for a job. The job I want is construction worker.

2 Fun with language

A Work with a partner. Talk about the pictures.

1. Is this **easy** or **difficult**?   2. Is this **boring** or **fun**?   3. Is this **dangerous** or **safe**?

B Work with a partner. Complete the chart. Use the words from Exercise A.

Occupation	Word to describe it
1. construction worker	*difficult*
2. salesperson	
3. housewife	
4. cashier	
5. pharmacist	
6. waiter / waitress	
7. hairstylist	
8. (your job) _____	

Work in a group. Talk about your opinions. Do you agree with your classmates? Why? Why not?

> I think a construction worker has a difficult job.

> I think a construction worker has a dangerous job.

> I agree. I think it's a dangerous job.

3 Wrap up

Complete the **Self-assessment** on page 144.

Review

1 Listening

Read the questions. Then listen and circle the answers.

1. What did Carlos do before?
   a. He was an office worker.
   b. He was a construction worker.

2. What does Carlos do now?
   a. He is an office worker.
   b. He is a construction worker.

3. When does Carlos buy groceries?
   a. every Tuesday
   b. every Thursday

4. Where is Carlos right now?
   a. at SaveMore Supermarket
   b. at work

5. What is he buying at the supermarket?
   a. milk, tea, bread, and eggs
   b. milk, cheese, bread, and eggs

6. How much are the groceries?
   a. $11.75
   b. $7.75

Talk with a partner. Ask and answer the questions. Use complete sentences.

2 Grammar

A Write. Complete the story.

Peter

Peter ___was___ a waiter in his country. Now he _____ a
     1. is / was   2. is / was

cashier. He can do many things. He _____ use a cash register.
                                  3. can / can't

He _____ use a computer, too. But Peter has two problems.
     4. can / can't

First, he _____ speak English well. Second, he works a lot of
        5. can / can't

hours. He _____ find time to go to school.
       6. can / can't

B Write. Unscramble the words. Make questions about the story.

1. a / teacher / Was / Peter / country / his / in / ? _Was Peter a teacher in his country?_

2. use / cash register / a / Can / he / ? _____

3. speak / well / English / Can / he / ? _____

4. he / construction worker / Is / now / a / ? _____

Talk with a partner. Ask and answer the questions.

3 Pronunciation: the -s ending with plural nouns

A 🔘 **Listen** to the -s ending in these plural nouns.

/s/	/z/	/ɪz/
cakes	tomatoes	peaches
hairstylists	electricians	nurses

B 🔘 **Listen and repeat.**

/s/	/z/	/ɪz/
assistants	bananas	nurses
cooks	cashiers	oranges
students	drivers	packages
mechanics	cookies	boxes
pharmacists	waiters	peaches
books	teachers	waitresses

Talk with a partner. Take turns. Practice the words. Make sentences with the words.

C 🔘 **Listen.** Complete the chart.

1. bags
2. bottles
3. clerks
4. dimes
5. pages
6. carrots
7. desks
8. sandwiches
9. glasses

/s/	/z/	/ɪz/
	bags	

D **Talk** with a partner. Ask and answer the question. Use correct pronunciation.

What's in your refrigerator?

There are _____ .   There is _____ .

Lesson A *Get ready*

1 Talk about the picture

A Look at the picture. What do you see?

B Point to a person: cleaning the bathroom • emptying the trash
mopping the floor • vacuuming the rug • ironing clothes

2 Listening

SELF-STUDY
AUDIO CD **A** 🔘 **Listen.** Circle the words you hear.

clean	mop	sweep
empty	paint	vacuum
iron	pay	(wash)

SELF-STUDY
AUDIO CD **B** 🔘 **Listen again.** Write the letter of the conversation.

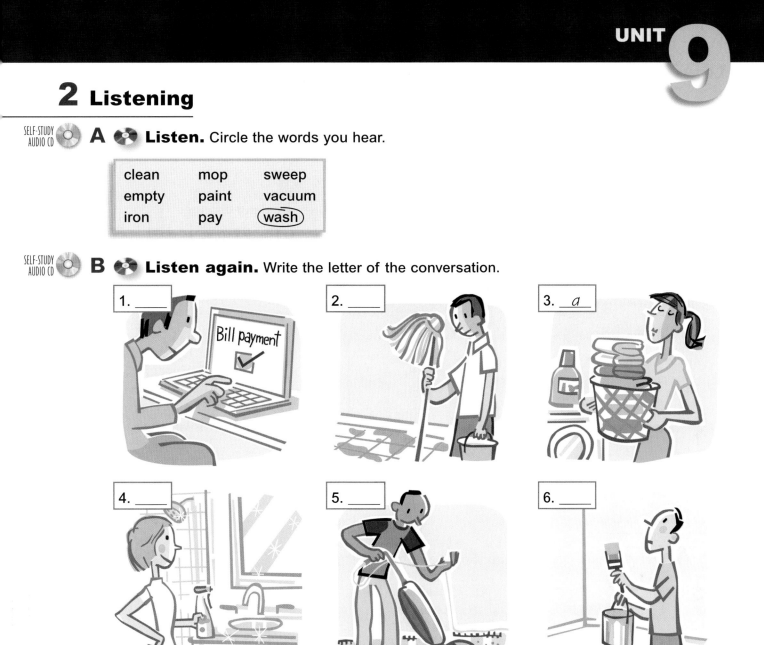

1. _____

Bill payment ✓

2. _____

3. _a_

4. _____

5. _____

6. _____

Listen again. Check your answers.

C **Write.** Work with a partner. Put the words from the box in the correct category.

a bill	the floor	a shirt	the trash
a dress	the rug	a ticket	the wastebasket

iron	empty	vacuum	pay
a dress			

I dusted the living room.

1 Grammar focus: simple past with regular verbs

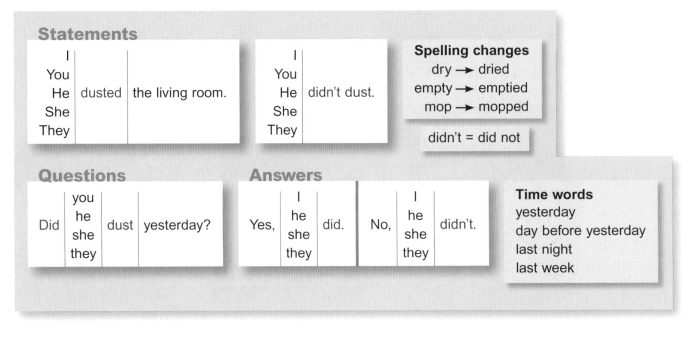

Statements

| I You He She They | dusted | the living room. |

| I You He She They | didn't dust. |

Spelling changes

dry ➝ dried
empty ➝ emptied
mop ➝ mopped

didn't = did not

Questions

| Did | you he she they | dust | yesterday? |

Answers

| Yes, | I he she they | did. |

| No, | I he she they | didn't. |

Time words
yesterday
day before yesterday
last night
last week

2 Practice

A Write. Look at the picture. Complete the sentences.

1. Yousef ___*cooked*___ dinner.
   (cook)

2. He __*didn't clean*__ the kitchen.
   (clean)

3. He _____ the shelves.
   (dust)

4. He _____ the dishes.
   (wash)

5. He _____ the shirts.
   (iron)

6. He _____ the trash.
   (empty)

Listen and repeat.

B Write. Look at the picture. Answer the questions.

Mr. Ramirez | Monica | Mrs. Ramirez | Luis | Roberto

1. **A** Did Mr. Ramirez mop the floor?
   B _Yes, he did._

2. **A** Did Mrs. Ramirez empty the trash?
   B _____

3. **A** Did Mr. and Mrs. Ramirez wash the dishes?
   B _____

4. **A** Did Roberto dry the dishes?
   B _____

5. **A** Did Luis vacuum the rug?
   B _____

6. **A** Did Monica vacuum the rug?
   B _____

Listen and repeat. Then practice with a partner.

3 Communicate

Talk with your classmates. Write their names in the chart.

Anna, did you cook dinner last night?   Yes, I did.

Find a classmate who:	Classmate's name
cooked dinner last night	
emptied the trash yesterday	
washed the dishes every night last week	
dried the dishes the day before yesterday	
vacuumed last weekend	
ironed clothes last week	

1 Grammar focus: simple past with irregular verbs

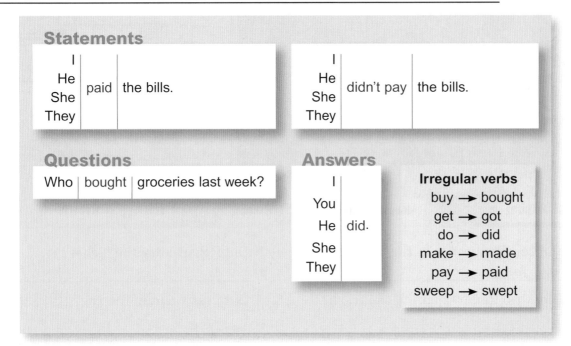

Statements

I		
He	paid	the bills.
She		
They		

I		
He	didn't pay	the bills.
She		
They		

Questions

Who	bought	groceries last week?

Answers

I	
You	
He	did.
She	
They	

Irregular verbs

buy → bought
get → got
do → did
make → made
pay → paid
sweep → swept

2 Practice

A Write. Look at the pictures. Complete the sentences.

Last night, Linda had to pay the bills. But first, she ____*bought*____ groceries after
1. buy

work. She _____ $15. She _____ home, and she _____
2. pay   3. get   4. make

dinner. She _____ soup and salad. After dinner, she was very tired. She
5. make

_____ the kitchen floor, but she _____ the bills!
6. sweep   7. not pay

Listen and check your answers.

B Write. Look at the notes. Answer the questions.

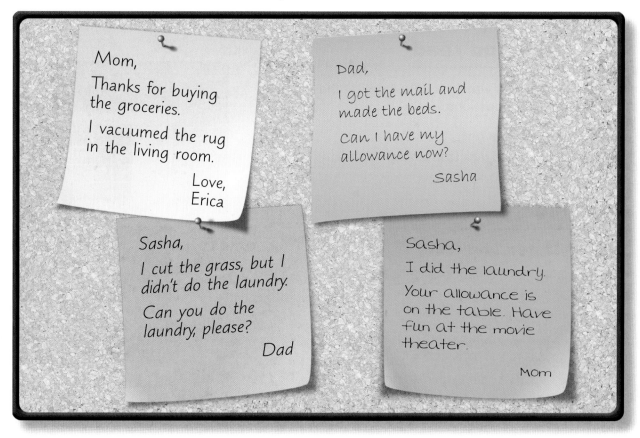

1. **A** Who bought the groceries?
   B _Mom did._

2. **A** Who made the beds?
   B _____

3. **A** Who vacuumed the rug?
   B _____

4. **A** Who got the mail?
   B _____

5. **A** Who cut the grass?
   B _____

6. **A** Who did the laundry?
   B _____

Listen and repeat. Then practice with a partner.

3 Communicate

Talk with a partner. What chores did you do yesterday? Check (✓) the boxes.

☐ paid the bills   ☐ did the laundry   ☐ swept the floor   ☐ washed the dishes
☐ bought the groceries   ☐ made the bed   ☐ got the mail   ☐ vacuumed the rug

Work in groups. Ask and answer questions.

Who paid the bills yesterday?   I did.   I didn't.

1 Before you read

Talk. Mark is writing a note. Look at the picture. Answer the questions.

1. Where is he?
2. What do you think Mark is writing about?

2 Read

SELF-STUDY
AUDIO CD

Listen and read.

Dear Karen,

Welcome home! We were very busy today. Jeff ironed the clothes. Chris emptied the trash. Sharon mopped the floor. Ben vacuumed the rug and dusted the furniture. The house is clean for you!

I cooked dinner. There is food on the stove.

Your husband,
Mark

Good readers ask themselves questions before they start reading, such as *Who wrote the letter?*

3 After you read

A **Read** the sentences. Are they correct? Circle *Yes* or *No*.

1. Jeff washed the clothes.	Yes	(No)
2. Sharon swept the floor.	Yes	No
3. Ben vacuumed the rug.	Yes	No
4. Karen cooked dinner.	Yes	No
5. Chris emptied the trash.	Yes	No

Write. Correct the sentences.

1. Jeff <u>ironed</u> the clothes.

B **Write.** Answer the questions about the note.

1. Who dusted the furniture? _____
2. Did Sharon empty the trash? _____
3. Who is Karen? _____

Picture dictionary   *Household objects*

1. ___*a sponge*___

2. _____

3. _____

4. _____

5. _____

6. _____

7. _____

8. _____

9. _____

SELF-STUDY
AUDIO CD

A 🔊 **Write** the words in the picture dictionary. Then listen and repeat.

a broom	an iron	a sponge
a bucket	a lawn mower	a stove
a dustpan	a mop	a vacuum cleaner

B Write. Match the objects with the actions.

1. an iron ___*d*___   a. vacuum

2. a sponge _____   b. sweep

3. a stove _____   c. mop

4. a lawn mower _____   d. iron

5. a mop _____   e. cook

6. a vacuum cleaner _____   f. wash

7. a broom _____   g. cut grass

Lesson E *Writing*

1 Before you write

A Talk with a partner. Ask and answer the questions.

1. Who does the chores in your home? What chores?
2. Are there special times to do those chores?
3. How do you feel about chores?

B Talk. Interview three classmates. Write two chores each person did last week and one chore they didn't do.

Name	Chores you did	Chores you didn't do
Katia	bought the groceries walked the dog	didn't vacuum the rugs

C Write. Complete the note. Use past tense forms of the verbs.

Dear Mom,

    I _____**bought**_____ milk from the supermarket. It's in the
              1. buy
refrigerator. I also _____ the shelves and _____
                         2. dust   3. sweep
the floor, but I didn't _____ the dishes. Did you
                        4. wash
_____ a new sponge? Did you _____ the rug
    5. buy   6. vacuum
yesterday? I also _____ my bed.
                    7. make

                                    See you later,

                                    Irina

D Write. Complete the note. Use the correct past tense form.

| buy | cook | dry | mop | pay | sweep | walk | wash |

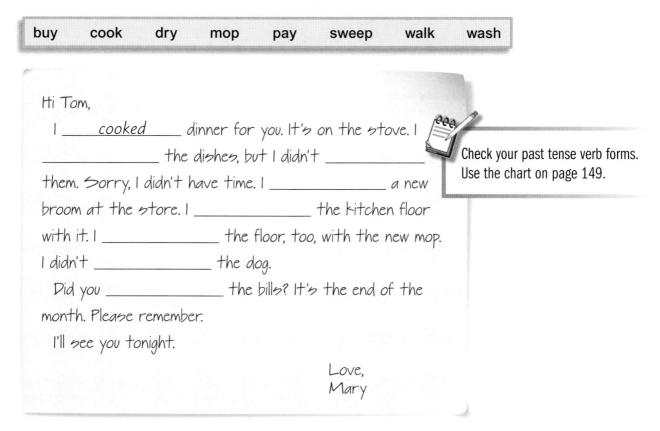

Hi Tom,

   I _____cooked_____ dinner for you. It's on the stove. I
_____ the dishes, but I didn't _____
them. Sorry, I didn't have time. I _____ a new
broom at the store. I _____ the kitchen floor
with it. I _____ the floor, too, with the new mop.
I didn't _____ the dog.
   Did you _____ the bills? It's the end of the
month. Please remember.
   I'll see you tonight.

                                  Love,
                                  Mary

Check your past tense verb forms.
Use the chart on page 149.

2 Write

Write a note to a family member. Write the chores you did and didn't do.

3 After you write

A Read your note to a partner.

B Check your partner's note.

- What are two chores your partner wrote about?
- Are the past tense forms correct?

1 Life-skills reading

JOB DUTIES			**SaveMore** Supermarket
Duties	**Employee**	**Initials**	**Time Completed**
Sweep the floor.	Joshua Liu	*JL*	*9:15 p.m.*
Mop the floor.	Kim Casey	*KC*	*9:30 p.m.*
Mop the floor.	Roger Brown	*RB*	*9:30 p.m.*
Clean the bathroom.	Ann Hamilton	*AH*	*8:30 p.m.*
Empty the trash cans.	Steve Johnson	*SJ*	*8:45 p.m.*
Turn off the lights.	Victor Morales	*VM*	*10:00 p.m.*
Lock the doors.	Victor Morales	*VM*	*10:00 p.m.*

A **Read** the questions. Look at the chart. Circle the answers.

1. Who swept the floor?
   a. Ann
   b. Victor
   c. Kim and Roger
   d. Joshua

2. When did Steve empty the trash cans?
   a. at 8:30 p.m.
   b. at 8:45 p.m.
   c. at 9:15 p.m.
   d. at 10:00 p.m.

3. Did Victor turn off the lights?
   a. Yes, he did.
   b. No, he didn't. He swept the floor.
   c. No, he didn't. He cleaned the bathroom.
   d. No, he didn't. He mopped the floor.

4. Who mopped the floor?
   a. Kim and Victor
   b. Steve and Joshua
   c. Ann and Roger
   d. Kim and Roger

B **Talk** with a partner. Ask and answer questions about the chart.

Who locked the doors? | Victor did.

Did Steve empty the trash? | Yes, he did.

2 Fun with language

A Work with a partner. What are these things? Write the words.

a broom	an iron	a mop	a stove
a dustpan	a lawn mower	a sponge	a vacuum cleaner

1. _an iron_   2. _____   3. _____   4. _____

5. _____   6. _____   7. _____   8. _____

B Work with a partner. Match.

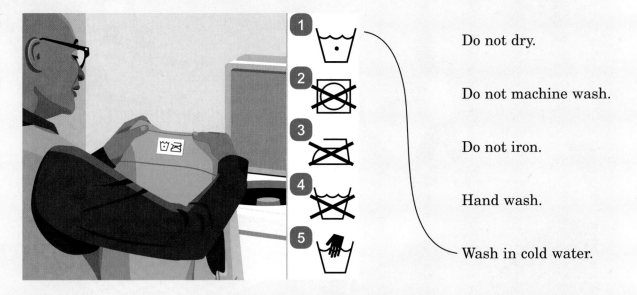

1   Do not dry.

2   Do not machine wash.

3   Do not iron.

4   Hand wash.

5   Wash in cold water.

3 Wrap up

Complete the **Self-assessment** on page 145.

Lesson A *Get ready*

1 Talk about the picture

A Look at the picture. What do you see?

B Point to these activities: camping • fishing • hiking • canoeing
swimming • picnicking

Mr. Lopez

Mrs. Lopez

What did you do yesterday?

Grammar focus: simple past with irregular verbs

Questions			Answers		Irregular verbs			
	did **you** do		I		drive → drove		ride → rode	
	did **he** do		He		eat → ate		see → saw	
What	did **she** do	yesterday?	She	went swimming.	go → went		sleep → slept	
	did **you** do		We		have → had		take → took	
	did **they** do		They		read → read		write → wrote	

Practice

A Write. Answer the questions.

1. **A** What **did** Mr. Brown do?
   B *He went fishing.*
   (go fishing)

2. **A** What did Carl do?
   B _____
   (go hiking)

3. **A** What did Gina do?
   B _____
   (go swimming)

4. **A** What **did** Mrs. Brown do?
   B _____
   (go riding)

5. **A** What did Carl and Gina do?
   B _____
   (go camping)

6. **A** What did Mr. and Mrs. Brown do?
   B _____
   (go canoeing)

Listen and repeat. Then practice with a partner.

2 Listening

SELF-STUDY AUDIO CD **A** 🔘 **Listen.** Circle the words you hear.

go camping	go hiking	play ball
go canoeing	go picnicking	read
go fishing	go swimming	rest

SELF-STUDY AUDIO CD **B** 🔘 **Listen again.** Write the letter of the conversation.

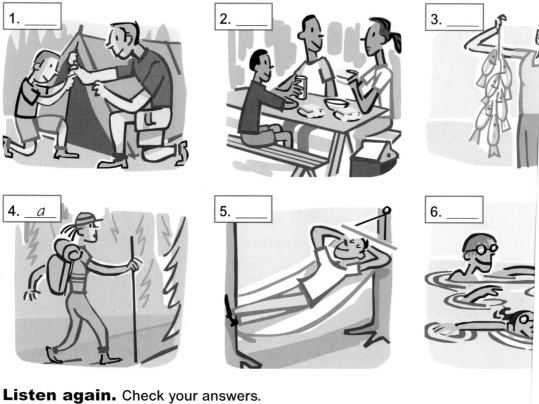

1. ____ 2. ____ 3. ____

4. _a_ 5. ____ 6. ____

Listen again. Check your answers.

C What do you do on your vacation? Check (✓) the boxes.

☐ go camping ☐ read books
☐ go fishing ☐ rest
☐ go hiking ☐ spend time with my family
☐ go swimming ☐ volunteer
☐ (other) _____ ☐ (other) _____

Talk with a partner. Ask and answer questions.

> What do you do on your vacation?

> I go hiking, swimming, and spend time with my family.

B **Write.** Complete the sentences. Use the correct past tense form.

eat	go	go swimming	ride	write

1. We _went swimming_ in the swimming pool last weekend.

2. I _____ my bike yesterday.

3. Silvia _____ e-mails to all her friends last week.

4. They _____ dinner very late last night.

5. We _____ picnicking last Sunday.

C **Talk** with a partner. Look at the schedule. Change the bold words and make conversations.

Jeff Yu's Vacation Schedule

Sun	Mon	Tues	Wed	Thurs	Fri	Sat
go to the museum	drive to the lake	ride my motorcycle	take swimming lessons	go hiking	go picnicking in the park	go to the movies

A What did Jeff do on **Sunday**?
B He **went to the museum**.

3 Communicate

Talk with three classmates. Complete the chart.

Sara, what did you do last night?   I read a book.

What did you do	Name:	Name:	Name:
last night?			
yesterday morning?			
the day before yesterday?			
last weekend?			

What are you going to do?

1 Grammar focus: future tense with *be going to*

Questions				
What	are you is he is she are they	going to	do tomorrow?

Answers			
I'm He's She's They're	going to	take a trip.

Time words
today
tomorrow
tonight
next week
next month

2 Practice

A Write. Read the schedule. Answer the questions.

1. **A** What's Marta going to do next Monday?

   B She's *going to take her exams* .

2. **A** What's Paco going to do next Tuesday?

   B He's _____ .

3. **A** What's Alfredo going to do next Wednesday?

   B He's _____ .

4. **A** What are Mr. and Mrs. Santiago going to do next Thursday?

   B They're _____ .

5. **A** What are Alfredo and Marta going to do next Friday?

   B They're _____ .

6. **A** What's the family going to do next weekend?

   B They're _____ .

Listen and repeat. Then practice with a partner.

Next Week's Schedule Santiago Family

Mon	Marta – take exams
Tues	Paco – play soccer
Wed	Alfredo – go hiking
Thurs	Dad and Mom – go swimming
Fri	Alfredo and Marta – go to a party
Sat & Sun	The family – take a trip

B Talk with a partner. Change the **bold** words and make conversations.

> **A** What**'s Brian** going to do today?
> **B He's going to go to the beach.**
> **A** That sounds like fun.

1. Brian / go to the beach
2. Ali / go shopping
3. Lisa / play soccer
4. Hiro and Lee / go fishing
5. Andrea / take a trip
6. Ray / go to a birthday party

> **Useful language**
> You can say:
> *I'm going to go fishing.* OR
> *I'm going fishing.*

3 Communicate

Talk to your classmates. Write their names and activities in the chart.

> Yuri, what are you going to do next weekend?

> I'm going to fix my car.

Name	Next weekend
Yuri	fix the car

Lesson D Reading

1 Before you read

Talk. Mrs. Lopez sent a picture of her family to a friend. Look at the picture. Answer the questions.

1. Who are the people in the picture?
2. What did they do?
3. What are they going to do next?

2 Read

SELF-STUDY AUDIO CD

Listen and read.

Dear Ming,

Last weekend, we went camping in the mountains. I went hiking. My husband and our sons went fishing. They also went swimming in the lake. We all had a great time!

Tonight we're going to eat fish for dinner. After dinner, we're going to watch a movie. Later tonight, we're going to be very busy. We are going to do the laundry. With three boys, we have a lot of dirty clothes!

See you soon,
Maria

> Look for words that show past or future time to help you understand.
> *Last weekend*
> *Tonight*

3 After you read

A Read the sentences. Are they correct? Circle *Yes* or *No*.

1. Last weekend, the Lopez family went shopping.	Yes	(No)
2. Mrs. Lopez went hiking.	Yes	No
3. Mr. Lopez and his wife went fishing.	Yes	No
4. The Lopez family is going to eat pizza for dinner.	Yes	No
5. After dinner, they are going to watch a movie.	Yes	No
6. They have a lot of clean clothes.	Yes	No

Write. Correct the sentences.

1. Last weekend, the Lopez family went <u>camping</u>.

B Write. Answer the questions about the Lopez family.

1. Who went fishing? _____

2. Who went swimming in the lake? _____

3. Is the Lopez family going to be busy tonight? _____

4 Picture dictionary Sports

1. _____football_____

2. _____

3. _____

4. _____

5. _____

6. _____

7. _____

8. _____

9. _____

SELF-STUDY
AUDIO CD

A ⊙ **Write** the words in the picture dictionary. Then listen and repeat.

Use *play* with these words:
baseball   football   Ping-Pong
basketball   ice hockey   soccer

Use *go* with these words:
ice-skating   skiing   surfing

B **Talk** with a partner. Look at the pictures and make conversations.

What's he going to do?   He's going to play football.

Culture note
In the United States, football and soccer are different sports.

1 Before you write

A Talk with four classmates. Ask questions. Write the answers.

> *A* Where did you go on your last vacation?
> *B* I went to Arizona.
> *A* Who did you go with?
> *B* I went with my wife.
> *A* What did you do?
> *B* We went to the Grand Canyon.

Name	Where?	Who with?	Did what?
Omar	Arizona	wife	visited the Grand Canyon

B Read Maria's note. Answer the questions.

Dear Colleen,
    I had a nice vacation. I went to Oregon. I went camping with my family. I read a book and rested. I went hiking. My husband and sons went fishing. We ate fish for dinner every night.
    Next year, we are going to drive to New York. We are going to visit my mother and see the Statue of Liberty.
    Did you have a nice vacation? What are you going to do on your next vacation?

             See you soon,
             Maria

1. Where did Maria go on vacation? *She went to Oregon.*

2. What did Maria do? _____

3. What did her husband and sons do? _____

4. Where is Maria's family going next year? _____

5. What are they going to do? _____

2 Write

A Write. Answer the questions.

1. Where did you go on your last vacation?

_____

_____

2. Who did you go with?

_____

_____

3. What did you do?

_____

_____

4. Where are you going to go on your next vacation?

_____

_____

5. Who will you go with?

_____

_____

6. What are you going to do?

_____

_____

B Write a letter about your vacations. Use the information from Exercise A.

Begin a new paragraph when you change your ideas from the past to the future.

3 After you write

A Read your letter to a partner.

B Check your partner's letter.

- What are the past activities?
- What are the future activities?
- Are there different paragraphs for past and future activities?

1 Life-skills reading

Saturday TV Schedule

	6:00	7:00	8:00	9:00
CHANNEL 7	Local news	Soccer		Swimming competition
CHANNEL 9	Cooking show	Boating program	*Great Places to Hike*	*Strange Animals*
CHANNEL 14	National news	Movie: *Camp Sunshine*		Kids' Favorite Vacations
CHANNEL 18	World news	*Fantastic Fishing*	Dancing competition	
CHANNEL 23	*Outdoor Adventures*	Baseball		

A Read the questions. Look at the TV schedule. Circle the answers.

1. On what channel are they going to show a movie?
   a. on Channel 9
   b. on Channel 14
   c. on Channel 18
   d. on Channel 23

2. When is *Outdoor Adventures* going to be on?
   a. at 6:00 p.m.
   b. at 7:00 p.m.
   c. at 8:00 p.m.
   d. at 9:00 p.m.

3. What are they going to show at 9 p.m. on Channel 9?
   a. *Great Places to Hike*
   b. *Kids' Favorite Vacations*
   c. *Fantastic Fishing*
   d. *Strange Animals*

4. How many channels are going to show the news at 6 p.m.?
   a. one channel
   b. two channels
   c. three channels
   d. five channels

B Talk with your classmates. Ask and answer the questions.

1. What did you watch on TV last night?
2. What are you going to watch on TV tomorrow night?
3. What are your favorite TV programs?
4. What do your family members watch on TV?

2 Fun with language

A Work in a group. What are you going to do next weekend? Do the activity in front of the group. Your classmates ask questions. Answer *Yes, I am* or *No, I'm not*.

> **A** Are you going to **go dancing** next weekend?
> **B** No, I'm not.
> **A** Are you going to **play soccer** next weekend?
> **B** Yes, I am.

B Work with a partner. Match the equipment with the sport.

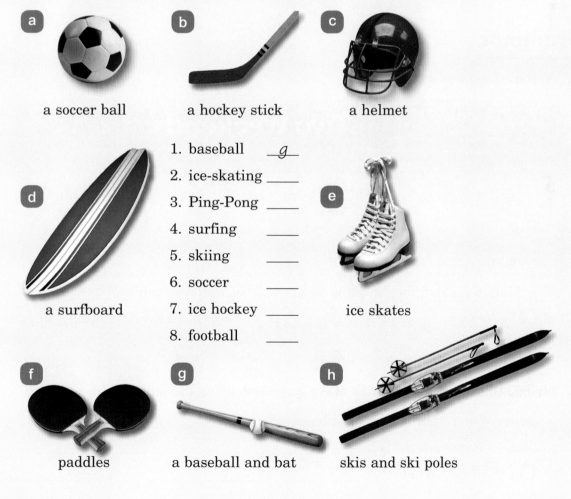

a · a soccer ball

b · a hockey stick

c · a helmet

d · a surfboard

e · ice skates

f · paddles

g · a baseball and bat

h · skis and ski poles

1. baseball ___g___
2. ice-skating _____
3. Ping-Pong _____
4. surfing _____
5. skiing _____
6. soccer _____
7. ice hockey _____
8. football _____

3 Wrap up

Complete the **Self-assessment** on page 145.

Review

1 Listening

🔘 **Read** the questions. Then listen and circle the answers.

1. When did Melissa's family go picnicking?
   a. on Saturday
   b. on Sunday

2. What did they eat in the park?
   a. hot dogs
   b. hamburgers

3. When did Ivan's family do their chores?
   a. on Saturday
   b. on Sunday

4. Did Ivan wash the dishes?
   a. Yes, he did.
   b. No, he didn't.

5. What did Ivan's wife do?
   a. She washed the clothes.
   b. She vacuumed the rugs.

6. Who dusted the furniture?
   a. Tommy
   b. Lisa

Talk with a partner. Ask and answer the questions. Use complete sentences.

2 Grammar

A Write. Complete the story.

Two Weekends

Sam and Jenny _____had_____ a big party last weekend. On Saturday morning,
            1. have / had

Jenny _____ the house and _____ dinner. Sam _____ the
       2. clean / cleaned   3. make / made   4. empty / emptied

trash and _____ the patio.
           5. sweep / swept

   Next weekend, they're going to _____ to the mountains. Sam is going
                                   6. drive / drove

to _____ fishing. Jenny is going to _____ swimming in a lake.
    7. go / went   8. go / went

B Write. Unscramble the words. Make questions about the story.

1. clean / When / Jenny / did / the house / ? _When did Jenny clean the house?_

2. dinner / Sam / make / Did / ? _____

3. Sam / do / did / What / ? _____

4. next / do / going to / they / What / are / weekend / ? _____

_____

Talk with a partner. Ask and answer the questions.

3 Pronunciation: the -ed ending in the simple past

A 🎧 **Listen** to the -ed ending in these past tense verbs.

/d/	/t/	/ɪd/
cleaned He cleaned his house.	**cooked** They cooked dinner.	**dusted** I dusted the living room.
dried I dried all the dishes.	**talked** She talked on the phone.	**folded** He folded his clothes.
emptied They emptied the trash.	**washed** She washed the car.	**painted** They painted the house.

B 🎧 **Listen and repeat.**

/d/	/t/	/ɪd/
exercised	camped	celebrated
played	fished	folded
turned	walked	visited

C 🎧 **Listen** and check (✓) the correct column.

	/d/	/t/	/ɪd/		/d/	/t/	/ɪd/
1. studied	✓	☐	☐	5. waited	☐	☐	☐
2. ironed	☐	☐	☐	6. hiked	☐	☐	☐
3. mopped	☐	☐	☐	7. vacuumed	☐	☐	☐
4. rested	☐	☐	☐	8. worked	☐	☐	☐

Talk with a partner. Take turns. Make a sentence with each verb.

D **Talk** with a partner. Ask and answer the questions. Use correct pronunciation.

1. What did you do last weekend?   2. What did you do yesterday?

Last weekend, I . . .

Yesterday, I . . .

Popular names

A Use the Internet.

Find popular names for girls and for boys.

Keywords | U.S. baby names | | popular names for girls | | popular names for boys |

B Make two lists.

Write 10 names for girls.
Write 10 names for boys.

C Share your information.

Make a class poster.
Write all the names from your lists.
Write the names in alphabetical order.
What are the class's favorite names?
Take a class vote.

Girls' names	Boys' names
1. Julie	1. Christopher
2. Sarah	2. Michael
3. Susan	3. Thomas

School employee chart

A Make a list.

What are some jobs at your school? Write the jobs.

B Talk to a school employee.

Ask these questions. Write the answers.
1. What's your first name?
2. What's your last name?
3. What's your title?
4. What's your job?

C Share your information.

Make a class wall chart.
Talk about the people.

Jobs at our school
1. teacher
2. principal
3. custodian

School employees

First name	Last name	Title	Job
Diego	Cruz	Dr.	Principal
Eve	Smith	Ms.	Secretary

Electronic greeting card

A Make a list.

Write the birthdays of eight people you know.
Who has the next birthday?
Circle the name.

Wang	July 10
Mr. Wilson	Aug. 21
Luz	Nov. 16

B Use the Internet.

Find a free electronic card.

Keywords | electronic cards | free e-cards | electronic birthday cards

Write a message.
Print a copy.
Send your card.

C Share your information.

Show the copy of the card to your classmates.

Health and emergency information

A Check (✓) the places and people that are important to you.

- ☐ Ambulance
- ☐ Emergency
- ☐ Fire Department
- ☐ Doctor
- ☐ Dentist
- ☐ Health Clinic
- ☐ Hospital
- ☐ Poison Control
- ☐ (other) _____

B Make an information card.

Write the important names on a card.
Find their phone numbers.
Write the numbers on the card.

Ambulance	911
Emergency	911
Doctor	555-1222
Dentist	555-9037
Health Clinic	555-1234

C Share your information.

Show your card to your classmates.
Add addresses and phone numbers
of other important places and people.

Projects

Community directory

A Use the Internet.

Find information about places in your community.

Keywords | (name of your town) | | (name of the place) |

B Make a chart.

Write addresses and phone numbers of important places.

Place	Address	Telephone number
Collinsville Museum	44 Maple Street	555-4589
Collinsville Public Library	12 Main Street	555-9023

C Share your information.

Show your chart. Talk about the places.

Business hours

A Make a list.

Write the names of three stores in your town.

B Make a chart.

Look for the stores in the telephone book.
Find the address and telephone number.
Then call. Ask these questions. Write the answers.
1. What days are you open?
2. What time do you open?
3. What time do you close?

C Share your information.

Make a wall chart.
Talk about the stores.

Store	Address	Telephone	Hours
ABC Grocery	2840 Main Street	555-6320	Tuesday – Saturday 7:00 a.m.–9:00 p.m. Sunday 8:00 a.m.–5:00 p.m.
Pam's Pizza	632 Garden Road	555-6789	Monday – Saturday 11:00 a.m.–11:00 p.m. Closed Sunday

Comparison shopping

A Write a one-week grocery list.

Include food, drinks, and other items you need.

B Find grocery ads from two stores.

Look in this week's paper or in the mail.
OR Go to the store to get the ad.

C Check the ads.

Write prices from each ad on your list.

D Share your information.

Show a classmate your grocery list.
Talk about the prices.
Which store is better for you?

Groceries	A&D Market	Ted's Food
bread	$1.99	?
milk	$2.50	?
bananas	59¢/lb	69¢/lb
lettuce	$1.50	?
onions	$1.29/lb	$1.19
potato chips	?	$2.49
soda	6/$2.00	6/$1.79
ice cream	$3.49	$3.79
toilet paper	6 rolls	8 rolls
	$4.00	$5.00

Job-description search

A Use the Internet.

Look for three jobs you want to learn about.

Keywords (name of job), job description   job description, (name of job)

B Find information about the jobs.

Look at the job descriptions.
Choose one job. Take notes.

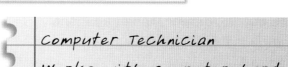

Computer Technician
Works with computer hardware,
software, and networks.

C Answer these questions.

1. What skills do you need for the job?
2. Do you need special training?
3. Do you need a degree or a certificate?
4. Is this job good for you?

D Share your information.

Find a picture of the job.
Paste it on a piece of paper.
Write information about the job.
Make a class booklet.

Projects

Time-management calendar

A Make a weekly calendar.

Use one or two sheets of notebook paper.

B Write on your calendar.

Write your work schedule.
Write your chores.
Write your study time.
Write other appointments or events.

C Share your information.

Show your calendar.
Talk about your schedule.

> **Monday**
> 7:00 make breakfast and lunches
> 8:15 take children to school
> 9:00 to 5:00 work
> 6:00 make dinner
> 7:00 wash dishes
> 9:00 put children to bed
> 10:30 study
>
> **Tuesday**
> 7:00 make breakfast and lunches
> 7:30 take out the garbage
> 8:15 take children to school
> 9:00 to 5:00 work
> 7:00 English class

Public parks

A Use the Internet.

Find the public parks near your home.

Keywords | local parks (your city) | public parks (your city) | recreation areas (your city)

B Take notes. Answer these questions.

1. What are the names of the parks?
2. What are the addresses of the parks?
3. What activities do they have there?

C Make a chart.

Write the information you found.

Name of park	Address	Activities
Solomon Park	First Avenue and Cherry Hill Road	bicycling, canoeing, swimming, picnicking

D Share your information.

Show your chart to the class.
Talk about your favorite park and the activities.

Self-assessments

Unit 1 Personal information

A Vocabulary Check (✓) the words you know.

☐ address	☐ city	☐ last name	☐ street
☐ apartment number	☐ country	☐ middle name	☐ telephone number
☐ area code	☐ first name	☐ state	☐ zip code

B Skills and functions Read the sentences. Check (✓) what you know.

I can use possessive adjectives: *What's **your** name? **My** name is _____ .*		I can read addresses with three or four numbers.	
I can use subject pronouns: *Is **she** from _____ ? Yes, **she** is. No, **she** isn't.*		I can complete a form with my personal information.	
I can begin names of people and places with capital letters.		I can list names in alphabetical order.	

C What's next? Choose one.

☐ I am ready for the unit test.   ☐ I need more practice with _____ .

Unit 2 At school

A Vocabulary Check (✓) the words you know.

☐ book	☐ chalkboard	☐ map	☐ pencil
☐ calculator	☐ desk	☐ marker	☐ ruler
☐ calendar	☐ eraser	☐ notebook	☐ stapler

B Skills and functions Read the sentences. Check (✓) what you know.

I can use the prepositions *in* and *on*: *It's **on** the _____ . It's **in** the _____ .*		I can read and understand an inventory list.	
I can use singular and plural nouns: *The **pen** is on the desk. The **pencils** are on the table.*		I can start sentences with a capital letter and end them with a period.	
I can look at a picture to help understand new words.		I can say ***excuse me*** to get someone's attention.	

C What's next? Choose one.

☐ I am ready for the unit test.   ☐ I need more practice with _____ .

Unit 3 Friends and family

A Vocabulary Check (✓) the words you know.

☐ aunt	☐ father	☐ husband	☐ son
☐ brother	☐ grandfather	☐ mother	☐ uncle
☐ daughter	☐ grandmother	☐ sister	☐ wife

B Skills and functions Read the sentences. Check (✓) what you know.

I can use the present continuous: *I am studying*.		I can use the title to understand a story.	
I can ask *yes / no* questions about the present: *Are you eating?*		I can spell the numbers from one to ten.	
I can identify family members.		I can read a form with personal information on it.	

C What's next? Choose one.

☐ I am ready for the unit test.   ☐ I need more practice with _____ .

Unit 4 Health

A Vocabulary Check (✓) the words you know.

☐ backache	☐ cough	☐ fever	☐ sore throat
☐ broken leg	☐ cut	☐ headache	☐ sprained ankle
☐ cold	☐ earache	☐ medicine	☐ stomachache

B Skills and functions Read the sentences. Check (✓) what you know.

I can use the simple present of *have*: *I have a headache. He has a cold.*		I can look for exclamation points when reading.	
I can ask questions with *have*: *Do you have a headache?*		I can write an excuse note about a sick child.	
I can write dates correctly.		I can read an appointment card.	

C What's next? Choose one.

☐ I am ready for the unit test.   ☐ I need more practice with _____ .

Unit 5 Around town

A Vocabulary Check (✓) the words you know.

- [ ] bank
- [ ] bus stop
- [ ] drugstore
- [ ] grocery store
- [ ] hospital
- [ ] library
- [ ] parking lot
- [ ] playground
- [ ] post office
- [ ] restaurant
- [ ] shopping mall
- [ ] train station

B Skills and functions Read the sentences. Check (✓) what you know.

I can use the prepositions *on*, *next to*, *across from*, *between*, and *on the corner of*.		I can give someone directions to places.	
I can use imperatives: *Turn right.* *Go straight* two blocks.		I can understand the pronouns (*I, he, it, they*) in a paragraph.	
I can read a map.		I can capitalize street names.	

C What's next? Choose one.

[ ] I am ready for the unit test.   [ ] I need more practice with _____ .

Unit 6 Time

A Vocabulary Check (✓) the words you know.

- [ ] buy
- [ ] drink
- [ ] eat
- [ ] get home
- [ ] leave for work
- [ ] read
- [ ] study
- [ ] take a break
- [ ] take a nap
- [ ] talk
- [ ] watch TV
- [ ] work

B Skills and functions Read the sentences. Check (✓) what you know.

I can use *at, in,* and *on* with time: *The meeting is in March. It is on Monday. It is at 1:00.*		I can ask questions to understand what I read: *Who, what, where, when?*	
I can ask *Wh-* questions about the present: *What does he do in the evening?*		I can indent when starting a paragraph.	
I can talk about daily activities: *I eat dinner in the evening.*		I can read a class schedule.	

C What's next? Choose one.

[ ] I am ready for the unit test.   [ ] I need more practice with _____ .

Unit 7 Shopping

A Vocabulary Check (✓) the words you know.

- ☐ apples
- ☐ bananas
- ☐ cashier
- ☐ check
- ☐ credit card
- ☐ dime
- ☐ nickel
- ☐ one-dollar bill
- ☐ penny
- ☐ quarter
- ☐ shopping cart
- ☐ supermarket

B Skills and functions Read the sentences. Check (✓) what you know.

I can ask questions using **How many** and **How much**: **How many** eggs do we have? **How much** coffee do we have?		I can make sentences using **There is** and **There are**: **There is** rice on the shelf. **There are** two boxes of tea on the shelf.	
I can find clues to understand new words.		I can use commas when listing three or more items.	
I can identify U.S. money.		I can read a shopping ad.	

C What's next? Choose one.

☐ I am ready for the unit test.   ☐ I need more practice with _____ .

Unit 8 Work

A Vocabulary Check (✓) the words you know.

- ☐ busboy
- ☐ cashier
- ☐ construction worker
- ☐ electrician
- ☐ housekeeper
- ☐ housewife
- ☐ nurse
- ☐ nursing assistant
- ☐ office worker
- ☐ receptionist
- ☐ salesperson
- ☐ truck driver

B Skills and functions Read the sentences. Check (✓) what you know.

I can use the simple past of **be**: **Were** you a student? Yes, I **was**. No, I **wasn't**.		I can understand past and present when I read.	
I can use **can**: He **can** cook. She **can't** drive a truck.		I can use a dictionary to check my spelling.	
I can write about my life skills and work skills.		I can complete an employment application.	

C What's next? Choose one.

☐ I am ready for the unit test.   ☐ I need more practice with _____ .

Unit 9 Daily living

A Vocabulary Check (✓) the words you know.

☐ broom	☐ dust	☐ mop	☐ sweep
☐ bucket	☐ empty	☐ paint	☐ vacuum
☐ do laundry	☐ iron	☐ pay the bills	☐ wash the dishes

B Skills and functions Read the sentences. Check (✓) what you know.

I can use the simple past with regular verbs: *They **dusted** yesterday. They **didn't** vacuum.*		I can use the simple past with irregular verbs: *She **paid** the bills. He **didn't make** dinner.*	
I can ask questions about what I am reading.		I can check my past tense verb forms when writing.	
I can read a note about daily chores.		I can read a job-duties chart.	

C What's next? Choose one.

☐ I am ready for the unit test.   ☐ I need more practice with _____ .

Unit 10 Leisure

A Vocabulary Check (✓) the words you know.

☐ baseball	☐ fishing	☐ ice-skating	☐ soccer
☐ basketball	☐ football	☐ picnicking	☐ surfing
☐ camping	☐ hiking	☐ skiing	☐ swimming

B Skills and functions Read the sentences. Check (✓) what you know.

I can talk about the past using irregular verbs: *What **did** you **do** last weekend? I **went** to the park.*		When I read, I can look for words that show time.	
I can talk about the future using **be going to**: *I **am going to** play soccer tomorrow.*		I can begin a new paragraph when changing from the past to the future tense.	
I can read a letter about a person's vacation.		I can read a TV schedule.	

C What's next? Choose one.

☐ I am ready for the unit test.   ☐ I need more practice with _____ .

Reference

Present of *be*

Affirmative statements

I'm	
You're	
He's	
She's	
It's	from Somalia.
We're	
You're	
They're	

I'm = I am		It's = It is
You're = You are		We're = We are
He's = He is		You're = You are
She's = She is		They're = They are

Yes / No questions

Am	I	
Are	you	
Is	he	
Is	she	
Is	it	from Guatemala?
Are	we	
Are	you	
Are	they	

Short answers

	you are.			you aren't.
	I am.			I'm not.
	he is.			he isn't.
Yes,	she is.		No,	she isn't.
	it is.			it isn't.
	you are.			you aren't.
	we are.			we aren't.
	they are.			they aren't.

Present continuous

Affirmative statements

I'm	
You're	
He's	
She's	
It's	eating.
We're	
You're	
They're	

Yes / No questions

Am	I	
Are	you	
Is	he	
Is	she	
Is	it	eating?
Are	we	
Are	you	
Are	they	

Short answers

	you are.			you aren't.
	I am.			I'm not.
	he is.			he isn't.
Yes,	she is.		No,	she isn't.
	it is.			it isn't.
	you are.			you aren't.
	we are.			we aren't.
	they are.			they aren't.

Wh- questions

	am	I	
	are	you	
	is	he	
	is	she	
What	is	it	doing?
	are	we	
	are	you	
	are	they	

Answers

You're	
I'm	
He's	
She's	
It's	eating.
You're	
We're	
They're	

Possessive adjectives

What's	my your his her its our your their	address?

Your My His Her Its Your Our Their	address is 10 Main Street.

Simple present

I	work.
You	work.
He	works.
She	works.
It	works.
We	work.
You	work.
They	work.

I	don't	
You	don't	
He	doesn't	
She	doesn't	work.
It	doesn't	
We	don't	
You	don't	
They	don't	

Do	I	
Do	you	
Does	he	
Does	she	work?
Does	it	
Do	we	
Do	you	
Do	they	

Yes,	you	do.
	I	do.
	he	does.
	she	does.
	it	does.
	you	do.
	we	do.
	they	do.

No,	you	don't.
	I	don't.
	he	doesn't.
	she	doesn't.
	it	doesn't.
	you	don't.
	we	don't.
	they	don't.

What	do	I	
	do	you	
	does	he	
	does	she	do at 7:00?
	does	it	
	do	we	
	do	you	
	do	they	

You	work.
I	work.
He	works.
She	works.
It	works.
You	work.
We	work.
They	work.

Simple present of *have*

Affirmative statements

I	have	a cold.
You	have	a cold.
He	has	a cold.
She	has	a cold.
It	has	a cold.
We	have	colds.
You	have	colds.
They	have	colds.

Negative statements

I	don't have	a cold.
You	don't have	a cold.
He	doesn't have	a cold.
She	doesn't have	a cold.
It	doesn't have	a cold.
We	don't have	colds.
You	don't have	colds.
They	don't have	colds.

Yes / No questions

Do	I		a cold?
Do	you		a cold?
Does	he		a cold?
Does	she	have	a cold?
Does	it		a cold?
Do	we		colds?
Do	you		colds?
Do	they		colds?

Short answers

	you	do.
	I	do.
	he	does.
	she	does.
Yes,	it	does.
	you	do.
	we	do.
	they	do.

	you	don't.
	I	don't.
	he	doesn't.
	she	doesn't.
No,	it	doesn't.
	you	don't.
	we	don't.
	they	don't.

Simple past of *be*

Affirmative statements

I	was	a teacher.
You	were	a teacher.
He	was	a teacher.
She	was	a teacher.
We	were	teachers.
You	were	teachers.
They	were	teachers.

Negative statements

I	wasn't	a cashier.
You	weren't	a cashier.
He	wasn't	a cashier.
She	wasn't	a cashier.
We	weren't	cashiers.
You	weren't	cashiers.
They	weren't	cashiers.

Yes / No questions

Was	I	a teacher?
Were	you	a teacher?
Was	he	a teacher?
Was	she	a teacher?
Were	we	teachers?
Were	you	teachers?
Were	they	teachers?

Short answers

	you	were.
	I	was.
	he	was.
Yes,	she	was.
	you	were.
	we	were.
	they	were.

	you	weren't.
	I	wasn't.
	he	wasn't.
No,	she	wasn't.
	you	weren't.
	we	weren't.
	they	weren't.

Simple past of regular and irregular verbs

Affirmative statements

I	
You	
He	
She	cooked.
It	slept.
We	
You	
They	

Negative statements

I		
You		
He		
She	didn't	cook.
It		sleep.
We		
You		
They		

Yes / No questions

	I	
	you	
	he	
Did	she	cook?
	it	sleep?
	we	
	you	
	they	

Short answers

	you				you	
	I				I	
	he				he	
Yes,	she	did.		No,	she	didn't.
	it				it	
	you				you	
	we				we	
	they				they	

Wh- questions

		I	
		you	
		he	
What	did	she	do?
		it	
		we	
		you	
		they	

Answers

You	
I	
He	
She	cooked.
It	slept.
You	
We	
They	

Regular verbs

Add -ed:
cook → cooked	talk → talked
dust → dusted	wash → washed

Irregular verbs

break → broke	get → got	ride → rode	sweep → swept
buy → bought	go → went	run → ran	swim → swam
do → did	have → had	see → saw	take → took
drink → drank	make → made	sell → sold	wear → wore
drive → drove	pay → paid	sit → sat	write → wrote
eat → ate	read → read	sleep → slept	

Can

Affirmative statements

I You He She It We You They	can	help.

Negative statements

I You He She It We You They	can't	help.

Yes / No questions

Can	I you he she it we you they	help?

Short answers

Yes,	you I he she it you we they	can.	No,	you I he she it you we they	can't.

Future – *be going to*

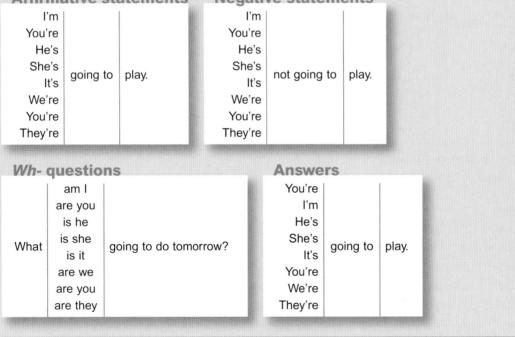

Affirmative statements

I'm You're He's She's It's We're You're They're	going to	play.

Negative statements

I'm You're He's She's It's We're You're They're	not going to	play.

Wh- questions

What	am I are you is he is she is it are we are you are they	going to do tomorrow?

Answers

You're I'm He's She's It's You're We're They're	going to	play.

Spelling rules

- Write out numbers from one to ten:
  We have six cans of soda.
- Use numbers for values 11 and higher:
  We have 11 cans of soda.
- Sentences and names start with capital letters:
  We live on Maple Street next to Mr. Smith.
- Verbs ending in *-y* take *-ied* in the simple past:
  dry → *dried*   *study* → *studied*
- Verbs ending in a vowel-consonant pair repeat the consonant in the simple past:
  mop → *mopped*

Punctuation rules

- Sentences can end with a period (.), question mark (?), or exclamation point (!):
  Simple statement: *We have soda.*
  Question: *Do we have soda?*
  Strong feeling: *We have soda!*
- Put a comma after every item but the last when a list has three or more items:
  We have soda, coffee, and water.
- Begin a new paragraph when you start a new topic or change the tense (time).
- Paragraphs start with an indent (space).

Cardinal numbers

0 zero	12 twelve	24 twenty-four	36 thirty-six
1 one	13 thirteen	25 twenty-five	37 thirty-seven
2 two	14 fourteen	26 twenty-six	38 thirty-eight
3 three	15 fifteen	27 twenty-seven	39 thirty-nine
4 four	16 sixteen	28 twenty-eight	40 forty
5 five	17 seventeen	29 twenty-nine	50 fifty
6 six	18 eighteen	30 thirty	60 sixty
7 seven	19 nineteen	31 thirty-one	70 seventy
8 eight	20 twenty	32 thirty-two	80 eighty
9 nine	21 twenty-one	33 thirty-three	90 ninety
10 ten	22 twenty-two	34 thirty-four	100 one hundred
11 eleven	23 twenty-three	35 thirty-five	1,000 one thousand

Ordinal numbers

1st first	9th ninth	17th seventeenth	25th twenty-fifth
2nd second	10th tenth	18th eighteenth	26th twenty-sixth
3rd third	11th eleventh	19th nineteenth	27th twenty-seventh
4th fourth	12th twelfth	20th twentieth	28th twenty-eighth
5th fifth	13th thirteenth	21st twenty-first	29th twenty-ninth
6th sixth	14th fourteenth	22nd twenty-second	30th thirtieth
7th seventh	15th fifteenth	23rd twenty-third	31st thirty-first
8th eighth	16th sixteenth	24th twenty-fourth	

Metric equivalents

1 inch = 25 millimeters	1 dry ounce = 28 grams	1 fluid ounce = 30 milliliters
1 foot = 30 centimeters	1 pound = .45 kilograms	1 quart = .95 liters
1 yard = .9 meters	1 mile = 1.6 kilometers	1 gallon = 3.8 liters

Converting Fahrenheit temperatures to Celsius

Subtract 30 and divide by 2: $80°F = 25°C$

Countries and nationalities

Afghanistan	Afghan	Brunei	Bruneian	Democratic Republic of the Congo	Congolese
Albania	Albanian	Bulgaria	Bulgarian		
Algeria	Algerian	Burkina Faso	Burkinabe		
Andorra	Andorran	Burundi	Burundian	Denmark	Danish
Angola	Angolan	Cambodia	Cambodian	Djibouti	Djiboutian
Argentina	Argentine	Cameroon	Cameroonian	Dominica	Dominican
Armenia	Armenian	Canada	Canadian	Dominican Republic	Dominican
Australia	Australian	Cape Verde	Cape Verdean		
Austria	Austrian	Central African Republic	Central African	East Timor	Timorese
Azerbaijan	Azerbaijani			Ecuador	Ecuadorian
Bahamas	Bahamian	Chad	Chadian	Egypt	Egyptian
Bahrain	Bahraini	Chile	Chilean	El Salvador	Salvadoran
Bangladesh	Bangladeshi	China	Chinese	Equatorial Guinea	Equatorial Guinean
Barbados	Barbadian	Colombia	Colombian		
Belarus	Belarussian	Comoros	Comoran	Eritrea	Eritrean
Belgium	Belgian	Costa Rica	Costa Rican	Estonia	Estonian
Belize	Belizean	Côte d'Ivoire	Ivoirian	Ethiopia	Ethiopian
Benin	Beninese	Croatia	Croatian	Fiji	Fijian
Bolivia	Bolivian	Cuba	Cuban	Finland	Finnish
Bosnia	Bosnian	Cyprus	Cypriot	France	French
Botswana	Motswana	Czech Republic	Czech	Gabon	Gabonese
Brazil	Brazilian			Gambia	Gambian

Georgia	Georgian	Malta	Maltese	Sierra Leone	Sierra Leonean
Germany	German	Marshall Islands	Marshallese	Singapore	Singaporean
Ghana	Ghanaian	Mauritania	Mauritanian	Slovakia	Slovak
Greece	Greek	Mauritius	Mauritian	Slovenia	Slovenian
Grenada	Grenadian	Mexico	Mexican	Solomon Islands	Solomon Islander
Guam	Guamanian	Micronesia	Micronesian	Somalia	Somali
Guatemala	Guatemalan	Moldova	Moldovan	South Africa	South African
Guinea	Guinean	Mongolia	Mongolian	South Korea	Korean
Guyana	Guyanese	Morocco	Moroccan	Spain	Spanish
Haiti	Haitian	Mozambique	Mozambican	Sri Lanka	Sri Lankan
Herzegovina	Herzegovinian	Namibia	Namibian	Sudan	Sudanese
Honduras	Honduran	Nepal	Nepali	Suriname	Surinamese
Hungary	Hungarian	Netherlands	Dutch	Swaziland	Swazi
India	Indian	New Zealand	New Zealander	Sweden	Swedish
Indonesia	Indonesian	Nicaragua	Nicaraguan	Switzerland	Swiss
Iran	Iranian	Niger	Nigerien	Syria	Syrian
Iraq	Iraqi	Nigeria	Nigerian	Tajikistan	Tajikistani
Ireland	Irish	Norway	Norwegian	Tanzania	Tanzanian
Israel	Israeli	Oman	Omani	Thailand	Thai
Italy	Italian	Pakistan	Pakistani	Togo	Togolese
Jamaica	Jamaican	Palau	Palauan	Tonga	Tongan
Japan	Japanese	Palestine	Palestinian	Trinidad	Trinidadian
Jordan	Jordanian	Panama	Panamanian	Tunisia	Tunisian
Kazakhstan	Kazakhstani	Paraguay	Paraguayan	Turkey	Turkish
Kenya	Kenyan	Peru	Peruvian	Turkmenistan	Turkmen
Kuwait	Kuwaiti	Philippines	Filipino	Uganda	Ugandan
Kyrgyzstan	Kyrgyzstani	Poland	Polish	Ukraine	Ukrainian
Laos	Laotian	Portugal	Portuguese	United Arab Emirates	Emirati
Latvia	Latvian	Puerto Rico	Puerto Rican	United Kingdom	British
Lebanon	Lebanese	Qatar	Qatari		
Lesotho	Basotho	Republic of the Congo	Congolese	United States	American
Liberia	Liberian			Uruguay	Uruguayan
Libya	Libyan	Romania	Romanian	Uzbekistan	Uzbekistani
Lithuania	Lithuanian	Russia	Russian	Venezuela	Venezuelan
Luxembourg	Luxembourger	Rwanda	Rwandan	Vietnam	Vietnamese
Macedonia	Macedonian	Samoa	Samoan	Yemen	Yemeni
Madagascar	Malagasy	Saudi Arabia	Saudi	Zambia	Zambian
Malawi	Malawian	Senegal	Senegalese	Zimbabwe	Zimbabwean
Malaysia	Malaysian	Serbia	Serbian		
Mali	Malian				

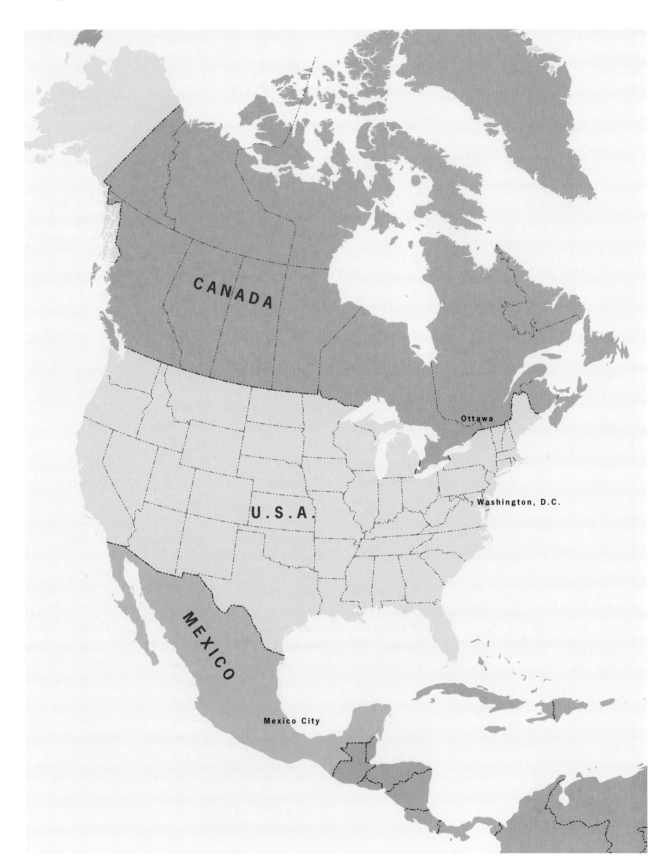

Self-study audio script

Welcome

Page 3, Exercise 2A – Track 2

A, B, C, D, E, F, G, H, I, J, K, L, M, N, O, P, Q, R, S, T, U, V, W, X, Y, Z

Page 3, Exercise 2C – Track 3

A What's your name?
B Helena.
A How do you spell that?
B H-E-L-E-N-A.

Page 4, Exercise 3A – Track 4

Zero, one, two, three, four, five, six, seven, eight, nine, ten, eleven, twelve, thirteen, fourteen, fifteen, sixteen, seventeen, eighteen, nineteen, twenty

Page 4, Exercise 3B – Track 5

1. six
2. twenty
3. one
4. fifteen
5. nine
6. twelve
7. nine
8. five
9. sixteen

Page 4, Exercise 3C – Track 6

1. three
2. eight
3. eighteen
4. twelve
5. one
6. zero
7. twenty
8. four
9. fifteen
10. eleven

Page 5, Exercise 4A – Track 7

Days: Sunday, Monday, Tuesday, Wednesday, Thursday, Friday, Saturday

Page 5, Exercise 4C – Track 8

Months: January, February, March, April, May, June, July, August, September, October, November, December

Unit 1: Personal information

Lesson A: Get ready

Page 7, Exercises 2A and 2B – Track 9

Conversation A
A What's your telephone number?
B My telephone number is 555-8907.

Conversation B
A What's your area code?
B My area code is 213.

Conversation C
A What's your last name?
B My last name is Clark.

Conversation D
A What's your address?
B My address is 1041 Main Street.

Conversation E
A What's your first name?
B My first name is Ricardo.

Conversation F
A What's your middle name?
B My middle name is Juan.

Lesson D: Reading

Page 12, Exercise 2 – Track 10

A New Student
    Svetlana Kulik is a new student. She is from Russia. Now she lives in Napa, California. Her address is 1041 Main Street. Her zip code is 94558. Her area code is 707. Her telephone number is 555-9073.

Page 13, Exercise 4A – Track 11

1. title
2. address
3. city
4. state
5. signature
6. zip code
7. apartment number
8. street
9. middle initial

Unit 2: At school

Lesson A: Get ready

Page 19, Exercises 2A and 2B – Track 12

Conversation A
A Where are the pens?
B They're in the drawer.

Conversation B
A Where is the calculator?
B It's on the desk.

Conversation C
A Where is the notebook?
B It's on the table.

Conversation D
A Is the map on the wall?
B Yes, it is.

Conversation E
A Are the rulers in the box?
B Yes, they are.

Conversation F
A Is the book on the chair?
B Yes, it is.

Lesson D: Reading

Page 24, Exercise 2 – Track 13

Attention, new students! Welcome to your new classroom.
The computer is on the small table.
The pencils are in the basket on the desk.
The erasers are in the basket.
The books are in the bookcase.
The calculators are on the bookcase.
The markers are in the desk drawer.

Page 25, Exercise 4A –
Track 14

1. chalk
2. notepads
3. bulletin board
4. chalkboard
5. index cards
6. stapler
7. paper clips
8. marker
9. globe

Unit 3: Friends and family

Lesson A: Get ready
Page 33, Exercises 2A and 2B –
Track 15

Conversation A
A Hello?
B Hi, Louisa. This is Mrs.
    Brown. Is your grandmother
    home?
A Yes, she is. She's watching TV.

Conversation B
A Hello?
B Hi, this is Mr. Cho. Is your
    father home?
A Yes, he is, but he's sleeping
    right now.

Conversation C
A Hello?
B Hi, Carlos. This is Mr. Ramos.
    Is your grandfather there?
A Yes, he is, but he's eating
    right now.

Conversation D
A Hello?
B Hi, this is Angela. Is your
    mother there?
A Yes, she is. But she's busy.
    She's cooking dinner.

Conversation E
A Hello?
B Hi, Carlos. This is Mary. Is
    your sister home?
A Yes, she is, but she's studying.

Conversation F
A Hello?
B Hello. This is Dr. Smith's
    office. Is your husband home?
A Yes, he is, but he's resting.

Lesson D: Reading
Page 38, Exercise 2 – Track 16

The Birthday Party
    My name is Juan. In this
picture, it's my birthday. I
am 70 years old. Look at me!
I don't look 70 years old. My
wife, my daughter, and my
grandson are eating cake. My
grandson is always hungry.
My granddaughter is drinking
soda. She's always thirsty. My
son-in-law is playing the guitar
and singing. Everyone is happy!

Page 39, Exercise 4A – Track 17

1. grandfather and grandmother
2. father and mother
3. aunt and uncle
4. brother and sister-in-law
5. husband and wife
6. cousin
7. niece and nephew

Unit 4: Health

Lesson A: Get ready
Page 45, Exercises 2A and 2B –
Track 18

Conversation A
A What's the matter?
B I have a headache.
A Oh, I'm sorry.

Conversation B
A What's the matter?
B I have a fever.
A Get some rest.

Conversation C
A What's the matter?
B I have a sprained ankle.
A Oh, I'm sorry.

Conversation D
A What's the matter?
B I have a stomachache.
A Oh, that's too bad.

Conversation E
A What's the matter?
B I have a sore throat.
A I hope you feel better.

Conversation F
A What's the matter?
B I have an earache.
A Oh, that's too bad.

Lesson D: Reading
Page 50, Exercise 2 – Track 19

The Health Clinic
    Poor Maria! Everyone is
sick! Maria and her children
are at the health clinic today.
Her son, Luis, has a sore throat.
Her daughter, Rosa, has a
stomachache. Her baby, Gabriel,
has an earache. Maria doesn't
have a sore throat. She doesn't
have a stomachache. And she
doesn't have an earache. But
Maria has a very bad headache!

Page 51, Exercise 4A – Track 20

1. eye	9. toe
2. ear	10. knee
3. back	11. finger
4. neck	12. hand
5. shoulder	13. chin
6. stomach	14. tooth
7. leg	15. nose
8. foot	16. head

Unit 5: Around town

Lesson A: Get ready
Page 59, Exercises 2A and 2B –
Track 21

Conversation A
A Excuse me. Where's the
    drugstore?
B The drugstore? It's on Fifth
    Avenue.

Conversation B
A Excuse me. Where's Low's
    Restaurant?
B Low's Restaurant? It's on
    Fifth Avenue. Go straight two
    blocks.

Conversation C
A Excuse me. Where's the
    post office?
B The post office is on Summit
    Street.

Conversation D
A Excuse me. Where's the museum?
B The museum? It's on Maple Avenue. Go straight one block.

Conversation E
A Excuse me. Where's the park?
B The park is on the corner of Maple and Summit.

Conversation F
A Excuse me. Where's the bus stop?
B The bus stop? It's on Orange Avenue. Go one block and turn left.

Lesson D: Reading
Page 64, Exercise 2 – Track 22

Hi Angela,

I love my new house. My neighborhood is great! Here are some pictures.

There is a school on my street. My children go to the school. They like it a lot. There is a community center across from the school. My husband works at the community center. He walks to work. There is a grocery store next to my house. It's a small store, but we can buy a lot of things. There is a good Mexican restaurant on Second Street. It's right across from my house.

I like it here, but I miss you. Please write.
Your friend,
Sandra

Page 65, Exercise 4A – Track 23

1. a shopping mall
2. a high school
3. a day-care center
4. a gas station
5. a playground
6. a police station
7. an apartment building
8. a hardware store
9. a courthouse

Unit 6: Time

Lesson A: Get ready
Page 71, Exercises 2A and 2B – Track 24

Conversation A
A Congratulations on your new job.
B Thanks.
A So when do you leave for work?
B I leave at ten-thirty.
A At night?
B Right.

Conversation B
A What time do you eat dinner?
B We eat dinner at six-thirty.

Conversation C
A What time do you start work?
B I start work at eleven o'clock at night.

Conversation D
A What time do you catch the bus?
B I catch the bus at ten-forty-five.

Conversation E
A What time do you take a break?
B I take a break at two-forty-five.

Conversation F
A What time do you get home?
B I get home around seven-thirty.
A In the morning?
B Right.

Lesson D: Reading
Page 76, Exercise 2 – Track 25

Meet Our New Employee:
Bob Green

Please welcome Bob. He is a new security guard. He works the night shift at the East End Factory. Bob starts work at 11:00 at night. He leaves work at 7:00 in the morning.

Bob likes these hours because he can spend time with his family. Bob says, "I eat breakfast with my wife, Arlene, and my son, Brett, at 7:30 every morning. I help Brett with his homework in the afternoon. I eat dinner with my family at 6:30. Then we watch TV. At 10:30, I go to work."

Congratulations to Bob on his new job!

Page 77, Exercise 4A – Track 26

1. eat lunch
2. take the children to school
3. walk the dog
4. take a shower
5. eat dinner
6. go to bed
7. get up
8. eat breakfast
9. get dressed

Unit 7: Shopping

Lesson A: Get ready
Page 85, Exercises 2A and 2B – Track 27

Conversation A
A We need some milk. Is there any milk on sale?
B Yes. Milk is a dollar eighty-nine.
A A dollar eighty-nine? That's cheap.
B How much do we need?
A A lot.

Conversation B
A We need some onions. Are there any onions on sale?
B Yes. Onions are seventy-nine cents each.
A Seventy-nine cents? That's expensive!
B How many do we need?
A Only one.

Conversation C
A We need some tomatoes. Are there any tomatoes on sale?
B Yes, tomatoes are eighty cents a pound.
A Eighty cents? That's cheap.
B How many do we need?
A A lot.

Conversation D

A We need some cheese. Is there any cheese on sale?

B Yes. Cheese is five ninety-nine a pound.

A Five ninety-nine? That's expensive!

B How much do we need?

A Not much.

Conversation E

A We need some potatoes. Are there any potatoes on sale?

B Yes. Potatoes are ninety-nine cents a pound.

A Ninety-nine cents? That's cheap.

B How many do we need?

A A lot.

Conversation F

A We need some bread. Is there any bread on sale?

B Yes, bread is three seventy-nine.

A Three seventy-nine? That's expensive!

B How much do we need?

A Not much.

Lesson D: Reading

Page 90, Exercise 2 – Track 28

Regular Customers

Shirley and Dan are regular customers at SaveMore Supermarket. They go to SaveMore three or four times a week. The cashiers and stock clerks at SaveMore know them and like them. There are fruit and vegetables, meat and fish, and cookies and cakes in the supermarket. But today, Shirley and Dan are buying apples, bananas, bread, and cheese. There is one problem. The total is $16.75. They only have a ten-dollar bill, 5 one-dollar bills, and three quarters!

Page 91, Exercise 4A – Track 29

1. a penny
2. a nickel
3. a dime
4. a quarter
5. a half-dollar
6. a one-dollar bill
7. a five-dollar bill
8. a ten-dollar bill
9. a twenty-dollar bill
10. a check
11. a credit card
12. an ATM card

Unit 8: Work

Lesson A: Get ready

Page 97, Exercises 2A and 2B – Track 30

Conversation A

A What does she do?

B She's a teacher.

A Really? What did she do before?

B She was a waitress.

Conversation B

A What does she do?

B She's a nurse.

A Really? What did she do before?

B She was a cook.

Conversation C

A What does she do?

B She's a doctor.

A What did she do before?

B She was a medical student.

Conversation D

A What does he do now?

B He's a busboy.

A What did he do before?

B He was a student.

Conversation E

A What does he do?

B Now? He's an electrician.

A What did he do before?

B He was a construction worker.

Conversation F

A What does he do?

B He's a manager at a restaurant.

A Really? What did he do before?

B He was a cashier.

Lesson D: Reading

Page 102, Exercise 2 – Track 31

Dear Ms. Carter:

I am writing this letter to recommend my student Mai Linh Lam.

Mai Linh was a teacher in Vietnam. She is looking for a new job in the United States. She is a certified nursing assistant now. She volunteers in a nursing home Monday through Friday from 8:30 to 4:30. She takes care of senior citizens.

Mai has many good work skills. She can write reports. She can help elderly people move around and sit down. She can help them eat. She can also speak English and Vietnamese. These skills are useful in her job, and she is very good at her work.

Sincerely,

Elaine Maxwell

Page 103, Exercise 4A – Track 32

1. housekeeper
2. custodian
3. pharmacist
4. factory worker
5. hairstylist
6. dental assistant

Unit 9: Daily living

Lesson A: Get ready

Page 111, Exercises 2A and 2B – Track 33

Conversation A

A Did you wash the clothes?

B Yes, I did.

A When?

B I washed them yesterday.

Conversation B

A Did you pay the bills?

B Yes, I did.

A When?

B I paid them last night.

Conversation C
A Did you clean the bathroom?
B Yes, I did.
A When?
B This morning.

Conversation D
A Did you vacuum the rug?
B No, I didn't.
A Please do it now.
B OK.

Conversation E
A Did you paint the wall?
B No, I didn't.
A Please do it now.
B OK.

Conversation F
A Did you mop the floor?
B No, I didn't.
A Please do it now.
B All right.

Lesson D: Reading
Page 116, Exercise 2 – Track 34

Dear Karen,
    Welcome home! We were very busy today. Jeff ironed the clothes. Chris emptied the trash. Sharon mopped the floor. Ben vacuumed the rug and dusted the furniture. The house is clean for you!
    I cooked dinner. There is food on the stove.
Your husband,
Mark

Page 117, Exercise 4A – Track 35

1. a sponge
2. a mop
3. a vacuum cleaner
4. a dustpan
5. an iron
6. a broom
7. a stove
8. a lawn mower
9. a bucket

Unit 10: Leisure

Lesson A: Get ready
Page 123, Exercises 2A and 2B – Track 36

Conversation A
A Hi, Diego!
B Oh! Hi, Carla. How are you? You look tired.
A Oh, no, I'm OK. I went hiking yesterday.
B Hey, I'm going to go hiking next weekend.

Conversation B
A Hi, Nicholas. How are you?
B Oh, pretty good. What's new with you?
A Well, we went camping last weekend.
B Really? We're going to go camping next month.

Conversation C
A Hey, Bill. How are you?
B Terrific. I was on vacation all last week.
A Really? What did you do?
B Nothing. I just needed to rest.

Conversation D
A Hi, Shawn. Where were you yesterday?
B I went with my family to Lookout Park. We went picnicking.
A Really? I'm going to go picnicking there next weekend.
B Well, watch out for the bees!

Conversation E
A Lidia, where were you yesterday?
B It was so hot we went swimming at the lake.
A Really? I'm going to go swimming next weekend.
B Have fun!

Conversation F
A Hey, Barbara, where did you get those fish?
B I went fishing this morning.
A Really? I'm going to go fishing tomorrow.
B Good luck.

Lesson D: Reading
Page 128, Exercise 2 – Track 37

Dear Ming,
    Last weekend, we went camping in the mountains. I went hiking. My husband and our sons went fishing. They also went swimming in the lake. We all had a great time!
    Tonight we're going to eat fish for dinner. After dinner, we're going to watch a movie. Later tonight, we're going to be very busy. We are going to do the laundry. With three boys, we have a lot of dirty clothes!
See you soon,
Maria

Page 129, Exercise 4A – Track 38

1. football
2. baseball
3. basketball
4. Ping-Pong
5. ice hockey
6. soccer
7. surfing
8. ice-skating
9. skiing

Illustration credits

Ken Batelman: 19, 59, 85, 89, 95 *(bottom)*

Cybele/Three in a Box: 37 *(top)*, 87

Travis Foster: 45 *(top)*, 78, 100, 111, 123

Chuck Gonzales: 17, 34, 35, 48, 95 *(top)*, 107, 112, 113

Stuart Holmes: 26, 68, 105

Ben Kirchner/Heart Agency: 2, 6, 7, 12, 14, 18, 24, 32, 33, 38, 44, 45 *(bottom)*, 50, 51 *(bottom)*, 58, 64, 70, 71, 76, 84, 90, 96, 102, 110, 116, 122, 128

Jim Kopp: 13, 25, 39, 51 *(top)*, 65, 77, 103, 117, 129

Mar Marube: 36, 37 *(bottom two)*

Frank Montagna: 11, 40, 55, 74, 124

Greg Paprocki: 21, 121, 127

Maria Rabinky: 60 *(bottom)*, 61, 63

Monika Roe: 22, 23, 27, 73, 92, 97, 114, 133

Photography credits

4 ©Fotosearch

5 ©Frank Veronsky

8 *(top)* ©Age fotostock; *(bottom, all)* ©Jupiter Images

9 ©Punchstock

15 ©Punchstock

20 *(all)* ©George Kerrigan

35 *(all)* ©Jupiter Images

46 *(top row, left to right)* ©Jupiter Images; ©Punchstock; ©Punchstock; *(middle row, left to right)* ©Veer; ©H.Benser/Zefa/Corbis; ©Age fotostock; *(bottom row, left to right)* ©David Young-Wolff/ Photo Edit; ©Photo Researchers; ©Jupiter Images

49 *(clockwise from top left)* ©Jupiter Images; ©Age fotostock; ©Age fotostock; ©Jupiter Images; ©Alamy; ©Alamy

69 *(left to right)* ©Jupiter Images; ©Istock; ©Istock; ©Jupiter Images

72 *(clockwise from top left)* ©Punchstock; ©Getty Images; ©Punchstock; ©Corbis

81 *(top to bottom)* ©Corbis; ©Getty Images

86 *(top row, all)* ©Jupiter Images; *(middle row)* ©Jupiter Images; ©Jupiter Images; ©Jupiter Images; ©Corbis; *(bottom row)* ©Jupiter Images; ©Jupiter Images; ©Punchstock; ©Punchstock

98 *(top to bottom)* ©Getty Images; ©Shutter Stock

99 *(clockwise from top left)* ©Bettmann/Corbis; ©Underwood Archives/Index Stock; ©John Firth/ Getty Images; ©H.Armstrong Roberts/Getty Images; ©Ewing Galloway/Index Stock; ©Corbis

101 *(clockwise from top left)* ©Corbis; ©Fotosearch; ©Punchstock; ©Superstock; ©Masterfile; ©Ed Bock/Corbis

121 *(clockwise from top left)* ©Punchstock; ©Jupiter Images; ©Jupiter Images; ©Jupiter Images; ©Jupiter Images; ©Corbis; ©Jupiter Images; ©Jupiter Images

131 *(both)* ©Corbis

133 *(clockwise from top left)* ©Jupiter Images; ©Corbis; ©Jupiter Images; ©Index Stock; ©Veer; ©Corbis; ©Corbis; ©Punchstock